QUOTES BY GREAT AMERICANS

*50 OF THE GREATEST AMERICANS QUOTATIONS TO
INSPIRE AND MOTIVATE*

M. PREFONTAINE

M. Prefontaine has asserted his moral right to be identified as the author of this work in accordance with the Copyright, Designs and Patents Act 1988.

Published by MP Publishing

INTRODUCTION

A list of the 50 Greatest Americans will inevitably be subjective and open to argument. There can be no defined parameters of greatness and the list would be ever changing as time goes on. How can we compare greatness and achievements in one field with those in another?

However, while it may well be that greatness is something that is difficult to define, I think we all know it when we see it. This list is simply my list, today.

It was William Shakespeare in Twelfth Night who said;

Some are born great, some achieve greatness and some have greatness thrust upon them.

There are some of all of these within this book. The purpose of the book is to provide a glimpse into the thinking and circumstances that made these people great, through their own words. Whether they were born great, achieved great things or lived in challenging times that demanded greatness can perhaps be seen through their thoughts which summarized their view of the world they were living in.

It is a glimpse into the minds and thinking of the people who molded the United States of America and made it the great country that it is today.

Contents

MUHAMMAD ALI

Muhammad Ali (1942 – 2016) was an Olympic boxing champion, subsequently he was world champion and considered by many the greatest boxer of all time. He converted to Islam and refused to serve in Vietnam. No one has straddled the world of sport, politics and popular culture as Ali did.

Friendship... is not something you learn in school. But if you haven't learned the meaning of friendship, you really haven't learned anything.

I hated every minute of training, but I said, 'Don't quit. Suffer now and live the rest of your life as a champion'

Float like a butterfly, sting like a bee. The hands can't hit what the eyes can't see.

He who is not courageous enough to take risks will accomplish nothing in life.

The word 'Islam' means 'peace.' The word 'Muslim' means 'one who surrenders to God.' But the press makes us seem like haters.

I know where I'm going and I know the truth, and I don't have to be what you want me to be. I'm free to be what I want.

If you even dream of beating me you'd better wake up and apologize. - GET REAL.

I done wrestled with an alligator, I done tussled with a whale; handcuffed lightning, thrown thunder in jail; only last week, I murdered a rock, injured a stone, hospitalized a brick; I'm so mean I make medicine sick.

I have been so great in boxing they had to create an image like Rocky, a white image on the screen, to counteract my image in the ring. America has to have its white images, no matter where it gets them. Jesus, Wonder Woman, Tarzan and Rocky.

Boxing is a lot of white men watching two black men beat each other up.

Only a man who knows what it is like to be defeated can reach down to the bottom of his soul and come up with the extra ounce of power it takes to win when the match is even.

If they can make penicillin out of mouldy bread, they can sure make something out of you.

People don't realize what they had till it's gone. Like President Kennedy, there was no one like him, the Beatles, and my man Elvis Presley. I was the Elvis of boxing.

Wars of nations are fought to change maps. But wars of poverty are fought to map change.

Anywhere I go, there is always an incredible crowd that follows me. In Rome, as I land at the airport, even the men kiss me. I love Rome.

I've made my share of mistakes along the way, but if I have changed even one life for the better, I haven't lived in vain.

Cassius Clay is a name that white people gave to my slave master. Now that I am free, that I don't belong anymore to anyone, that I'm not a slave anymore, I gave back their white name, and I chose a beautiful African one.

I'm the greatest thing that ever lived! I'm the king of the world! I'm a bad man. I'm the prettiest thing that ever lived.

Never put your money against Cassius Clay, for you will never have a lucky day.

I figured that if I said it enough, I would convince the world that I really was the greatest.

To be able to give away riches is mandatory if you wish to possess them. This is the only way that you will be truly rich.

Joe Frazier is so ugly that when he cries, the tears turn around and go down the back of his head.

No one knows what to say in the loser's locker room.

When you can whip any man in the world, you never know peace.

I always bring out the best in men I fight, but Joe Frazier, I'll tell the world right now, brings out the best in me. I'm gonna tell ya, that's one helluva man, and God bless him.

Frazier is so ugly that he should donate his face to the U.S. Bureau of Wild Life.

The fight is won or lost far away from witnesses - behind the lines, in the gym, and out there on the road, long before I dance under those lights.

 Terrorists are not following Islam. Killing people and blowing up people and dropping bombs in places and all this is not the way to spread the word of Islam. So people realize now that all Muslims are not terrorists. **JUDGMENT**

 It isn't the mountains ahead to climb that wear you out; it's the pebble in your shoe. **SMALL STUFF**

The man who has no imagination has no wings.

Life is a gamble. You can get hurt, but people die in plane crashes, lose their arms and legs in car accidents; people die every day. Same with fighters: some die, some get hurt, some go on. You just don't let yourself believe it will happen to you.

I'm so fast that last night I turned off the light switch in my hotel room and was in bed before the room was dark.

 A man who views the world the same at fifty as he did at twenty has wasted thirty years of his life. CHANGE

Rivers, ponds, lakes and streams - they all have different names, but they all contain water. Just as religions do - they all contain truths.

It's the repetition of affirmations that leads to belief. And once that belief becomes a deep conviction, things begin to happen.

I'm the most recognized and loved man that ever lived cuz there weren't no satellites when Jesus and Moses were around, so people far away in the villages didn't know about them.

It's just a job. Grass grows, birds fly, waves pound the sand. I beat people up.

I wish people would love everybody else the way they love me. It would be a better world.

My principles are more important than the money or my title.

 Hating people because of their color is wrong. And it doesn't matter which color does the hating. It's just plain wrong. RACISM

If you lose a big fight, it will worry you all of your life. It will plague you - until you get your revenge.

 Service to others is the rent you pay for your room here on earth.

I should be a postage stamp, because that's the only way I'll ever get licked. I'm beautiful. I'm fast. I'm so mean I make medicine sick. I can't possibly be beat.

 SERVING WHO?

4

Ali's got a left, Ali's got a right - when he knocks you down, you'll sleep for the night; and when you lie on the floor and the ref counts to ten, hope and pray that you never meet me again.

Old age is just a record of one's whole life.

You think the world was shocked when Nixon resigned? Wait till I whup George Foreman's behind.

I'm just hoping that people understand that Islam is peace and not violence.

I'll beat him so bad he'll need a shoehorn to put his hat on.

There are more pleasant things to do than beat up people.

I figure I'll be champ for about ten years and then I'll let my brother take over - like the Kennedys down in Washington.

If I said I would knock out Sonny Liston in 1 minute and 49 seconds of the first round, that would hurt the gate.

I know I got it made while the masses of black people are catchin' hell, but as long as they ain't free, I ain't free.

I got no quarrel with them Vietcong

I didn't want to submit to the army and then, on the day of judgment, have God say to me, 'Why did you do that?' This life is a trial, and you realize that what you do is going to be written down for Judgment Day.

To be a great champion you must believe you are the best. If you're not, pretend you are.

MAYA ANGELOU

Maya Angelou (1928 – 2014) was a poet, author, actress and civil rights activist who is best known for her seven autobiographies in which she wrote of her rise from poverty and violence to become a renowned and inspirational spokeswoman for both black people and women.

If you don't like something, change it. If you can't change it, change your attitude.

If you're always trying to be normal you will never know how amazing you can be.

Try to be a rainbow in someone's cloud.

I've learned that people will forget what you said, people will forget what you did, but people will never forget how you made them feel.

History, despite its wrenching pain, cannot be unlived, but if faced with courage, need not be lived again. ‒ PRIGHTESS?

The ache for home lives in all of us, the safe place where we can go as we are and not be questioned.

Music was my refuge. I could crawl into the space between the notes and curl my back to loneliness.

A wise woman wishes to be no one's enemy; a wise woman refuses to be anyone's victim.

It is time for parents to teach young people early on that in diversity there is beauty and there is strength.

There is no greater agony than bearing an untold story inside you.

#9 - FEAR

Courage is the most important of all the virtues because without courage, you can't practice any other virtue consistently.

You may not control all the events that happen to you, but you can decide not to be reduced by them.

Never make someone a priority when all you are to them is an option.

Ask for what you want and be prepared to get it!

Bitterness is like cancer. It eats upon the host. But anger is like fire. It burns it all clean.

Most people don't grow up. Most people age. They find parking spaces, honor their credit cards, get married, have children, and call that maturity. What that is, is aging.

There's a world of difference between truth and facts. Facts can obscure truth.

I've learned that you can tell a lot about a person by the way (s)he handles these three things: a rainy day, lost luggage, and tangled Christmas tree lights.

You can only become truly accomplished at something you love. Don't make money your goal. Instead pursue the things you love doing and then do them so well that people can't take their eyes off of you.

#10 Love of country
Love recognizes no barriers. It jumps hurdles, leaps fences, penetrates walls to arrive at its destination full of hope.

Life is not measured by the number of breaths you take but by the moments that take your breath away

You can't use up creativity. The more you use, the more you have.

I've learned that making a living is not the same thing as making a life.

I have found that among its other benefits, giving liberates the soul of the giver.

TAKERS

SUSAN B ANTHONY

Susan B Anthony (1820 -1906) was a women's right activist and a social reformer who played a critical role in the advancement of women's rights. Although she did not live to see women get the vote the Nineteenth Amendment, which gave women the vote in 1920, was popularly known as the Anthony amendment.

I declare to you that woman must not depend upon the protection of man, but must be taught to protect herself, and there I take my stand.

The older I get, the greater power I seem to have to help the world; I am like a snowball - the further I am rolled the more I gain.

Cautious, careful people, always casting about to preserve their reputations... can never effect a reform.

I always distrust people who know so much about what God wants them to do to their fellows.

I beg you to speak of Woman as you do of the Negro, speak of her as a human being, as a citizen of the United States, as a half of the people in whose hands lies the destiny of this Nation.

I do not consider divorce an evil by any means. It is just as much a refuge for women married to brutal men as Canada was to the slaves of brutal masters.

I don't want to die as long as I can work; the minute I cannot, I want to go.

I have encountered riotous mobs and have been hung in effigy, but my motto is: Men's rights are nothing more. Women's rights are nothing less.

EQUALITY SO DIFFICULT?

9

I shall earnestly and persistently continue to urge all women to the practical recognition of the old Revolutionary maxim. Resistance to tyranny is obedience to God.

I think the girl who is able to earn her own living and pay her own way should be as happy as anybody on earth. The sense of independence and security is very sweet.

If all the rich and all of the church people should send their children to the public schools, they would feel bound to concentrate their money on improving these schools until they met the highest ideals.

Independence is happiness.

Modern invention has banished the spinning wheel, and the same law of progress makes the woman of today a different woman from her grandmother.

No man is good enough to govern any woman without her consent.

Trust me that as I ignore all law to help the slave, so will I ignore it all to protect an enslaved woman.

Let me tell you what I think of bicycling. I think it has done more to emancipate women than anything else in the world. It gives women a feeling of freedom and self—reliance. I stand and rejoice every time I see a woman ride by on a wheel...the picture of free, untrammeled womanhood.

Whoever controls work and wages, controls morals.

The day may be approaching when the whole world will recognize woman as the equal of man.

Suffrage is the pivotal right.

Oh, if I could but live another century and see the fruition of all the work for women. There is so much yet to be done.

You would better educate ten women into the practice of liberal principles than to organize a thousand on a platform of intolerance and bigotry.

Women, we might as well be dogs baying the moon as petitioners without the right to vote.

I will cut off this right arm of mine before I will ask for the ballot for the Negro and not for the woman.

Join the union, girls, and together say Equal Pay for Equal Work.

This is rather different from the receptions I used to get fifty years ago. They threw things at me then but they were not roses.

Resolved, that the women of this nation in 1876, have greater cause for discontent, rebellion and revolution than the men of 1776.

The worst enemy women have is in the pulpit.

To think, I have had more than 60 years of hard struggle for a little liberty, and then to die without it seems so cruel.

Organize, agitate, educate, must be our war cry.

White men have always controlled their wives' wages. Colored men were not able to do so until they themselves became free. Then they owned both their wives and their wages.

MARLON BRANDO

Marlon Brando (1924 – 2004) was an actor, a film director and a political activist. He was known as a particularly influential gritty and realistic actor. He was an advocate of civil rights in particular of the Native Americans.

The only thing an actor owes his public is not to bore them.

An actor is at most a poet and at least an entertainer.

Privacy is not something that I'm merely entitled to, it's an absolute prerequisite.

Never confuse the size of your paycheck with the size of your talent.

I value each woman for what she has to offer whether it be charm-beauty-wit-intelligence or humor but warmth is the quality I value most.

Never surrender to the momentum of mediocrity.

I watched a snail crawl along the edge of a straight razor. That's my dream. That's my nightmare. Crawling, slithering, along the edge of a straight razor and surviving.

In a close-up, the audience is only inches away, and your face becomes the stage.

An actor's a guy who, if you ain't talking about him, ain't listening.

The principal benefit acting has afforded me is the money to pay for my psychoanalysis.

When they laid down their arms, we murdered them. We lied to them. We cheated them out of their lands. We starved them into signing fraudulent agreements that we called treaties which we never kept. We turned them into beggars on a continent that gave life for as long as life can remember. And by any interpretation of history, however twisted, we did not do right.

The only reason I'm in Hollywood is that I don't have the moral courage to refuse the money.

Acting is an empty and useless profession.

You can sit there and have a universal experience, of fear, of anger, of tears, of love, and I discovered that it's the audience, really, that is doing the acting.

To grasp the full significance of life is the actor's duty, to interpret it is his problem, and to express it his dedication.

I think awards in this country at this time are inappropriate to be received or given until the condition of the American Indian is drastically altered. If we are not our brother's keeper, at least let us not be his executioner.

If you want something from an audience, you give blood to their fantasies. It's the ultimate hustle.

The four pillars of wisdom that support journalistic endeavors are: lies, stupidity, money-grubbing, and ethical irresponsibility.

It's a long climb up Fools' Hill. — STILL HOPE

If you're successful, acting is about as soft a job as anybody could ever wish for. But if you're unsuccessful it's worse than having a skin disease.

It's the hardest thing in the world to accept a 'little' success and leave it that way.

WARREN BUFFET

Warren Buffet (1932 -) is an investor and philanthropist widely known as 'The Sage of Omaha'. He is the Chairman and CEO of Berkshire Hathaway, an investment company. He is an advocate of 'value investing' and is amongst the richest men in the world. He has pledged to give 99% of his wealth to charity.

I never attempt to make money on the stock market. I buy on the assumption that they could close the market the next day and not reopen it for five years.

 You only have to do a very few things right in your life so long as you don't do too many things wrong.

Should you find yourself in a chronically leaking boat, energy devoted to changing vessels is likely to be a more productive than energy devoted to patching leaks.

 It is not necessary to do extraordinary things to get extraordinary results. *EXCEPTIONAL*

What we learn from history is that people don't learn from history.

Chains of habit are too light to be felt until they are too heavy to be broken.

 There seems to be some perverse human characteristic that likes to make easy things difficult. *NEATEN UP*

Nothing sedates rationality like large doses of effortless money.

It takes 20 years to build a reputation and five minutes to ruin it. If you think about that, you'll do things differently.

It's better to hang out with people better than you. Pick out associates whose behavior is better than yours and you'll drift in that direction.

Long ago, Ben Graham taught me that 'Price is what you pay; value is what you get.' Whether we're talking about socks or stocks, I like buying quality merchandise when it is marked down.

The most important quality for an investor is temperament, not intellect. You need a temperament that neither derives great pleasure from being with the crowd or against the crowd.

Successful Investing takes time, discipline and patience. No matter how great the talent or effort, some things just take time: You can't produce a baby in one month by getting nine women pregnant.

I don't look to jump over seven-foot bars; I look around for one-foot bars that I can step over.

In the short term, the market is a popularity contest. In the long term, the market is a weighing machine.

Opportunities come infrequently. When it rains gold, put out the bucket, not the thimble.

Diversification is a protection against ignorance. It makes very little sense for those who know what they're doing.

If you aren't willing to own a stock for ten years, don't even think about owning it for ten minutes. Put together a portfolio of companies whose aggregate earnings march upward over the years, and so also will the portfolio's market value.

The key to investing is not assessing how much an industry is going to affect society, or how much it will grow, but rather determining the competitive advantage of any given company and, above all, the durability of that advantage.

I am a better investor because I am a businessman, and a better businessman because I am an investor.

It's far better to buy a wonderful company at a fair price than a fair company at a wonderful price.

In the business world, the rearview mirror is always clearer than the windshield.

Risk comes from not knowing what you're doing.

Only when the tide goes out do you discover who's been swimming naked

A public-opinion poll is no substitute for thought.

The business schools reward difficult complex behavior more than simple behavior, but simple behavior is more effective.

Look at market fluctuations as your friend rather than your enemy; profit from folly rather than participate in it.

Of the billionaires I have known, money just brings out the basic traits in them. If they were jerks before they had money, they are simply jerks with a billion dollars.

If past history was all there was to the game, the richest people would be librarians.

The smarter the journalists are, the better off society is. [For] to a degree, people read the press to inform themselves-and the better the teacher, the better the student body.

You do things when the opportunities come along. I've had periods in my life when I've had a bundle of ideas come along, and I've had long dry spells. If I get an idea next week, I'll do something. If not, I won't do a damn thing.

The only time to buy these is on a day with no 'y' in it.

We simply attempt to be fearful when others are greedy and to be greedy only when others are fearful.

Time is the friend of the wonderful company, the enemy of the mediocre.

Somebody is sitting in the shade today because someone planted a tree a long time ago.

SHIRLEY CHISHOLM

Shirley Chisholm (1924 – 2005) was a politician, author and educator. She was the first African American woman to be elected to congress in 1968, and subsequently became the first African American candidate to be President from a major party.

At present, our country needs women's idealism and determination, perhaps more in politics than anywhere else.

Congress seems drugged and inert most of the time... its idea of meeting a problem is to hold hearings or, in extreme cases, to appoint a commission.

Service is the rent that you pay for room on this earth.

You don't make progress by standing on the sidelines, whimpering and complaining. You make progress by implementing ideas.

Tremendous amounts of talent are lost to our society just because that talent wears a skirt.

Of my two handicaps, being female put many more obstacles in my path than being black.

The emotional, sexual, and psychological stereotyping of females begins when the doctor says: It's a girl.

When morality comes up against profit, it is seldom that profit loses.

There is little place in the political scheme of things for an independent, creative personality, for a fighter. Anyone who takes that role must pay a price.

 I don't measure America by its achievement but by its potential.

18

All we want is what you want, no less and no more.

Take away an accident of pigmentation of a thin layer of our outer skin and there is no difference between me and anyone else. All we want is for that trivial difference to make no difference. What can I say to a man who asks that?

I am not anti-white, because I understand that white people, like black ones, are victims of a racist society. They are products of their time and place.

In the end anti-black, anti-female, and all forms of discrimination are equivalent to the same thing – anti-humanism.

It is not heroin or cocaine that makes one an addict, it is the need to escape from a harsh reality. There are more television addicts, more baseball and football addicts, more movie addicts, and certainly more alcohol addicts in this country than there are narcotics addicts.

Racism is so universal in this country, so widespread, and deep-seated, that it is invisible because it is so normal

Rhetoric never won a revolution yet.

The liberals in the House strongly resemble liberals I have known through the last two decades in the civil rights conflict. When it comes time to show on which side they will be counted, they excuse themselves.

The one thing you've got going: your one vote.

To label family planning and legal abortion programs "genocide" is male rhetoric, for male ears.

We Americans have a chance to become someday a nation in which all racial stocks and classes can exist in their own selfhoods, but

19

meet on a basis of respect and equality and live together, socially, economically, and politically.

Women know, and so do many men, that two or three children who are wanted, prepared for, reared amid love and stability, and educated to the limit of their ability will mean more for the future of the black and brown races from which they come than any number of neglected, hungry, ill-housed and ill-clothed youngsters. Pride in one's race, as will simple humanity, supports this view.

Defeat should not be the source of discouragement, but a stimulus to keep plotting.

Don't listen to those who say 'you can't'. Listen to the voice inside yourself that says, 'I can'.

As there were no black Founding Fathers, there were no founding mothers - a great pity on both counts.

The difference between de jure and de facto segregation is the difference between open, forthright bigotry and the shamefaced kind that works through unwritten agreements between real estate dealers, school officials, and local politicians.

We have never seen health as a right. It has been conceived as a privilege, available only to those who can afford it. This is the real reason the American health care system is in such a scandalous state.

Some fine men are in Congress, too few, trying to do a responsible job. But they are surrounded and almost neutralized by a greater number whose instinct is to make a deal before they make a decision.

I ran for the presidency, despite hopeless odds, to demonstrate the sheer will and refusal to accept the status quo... to give a voice to the people the major candidates were ignoring. What I hope most is that now there will be others who will feel themselves as capable of running for high political office as any wealthy, good-looking white male.

Laws will not eliminate prejudice from the hearts of human beings. But that is no reason to allow prejudice to continue to be enshrined in our laws to perpetuate injustice through inaction.

Noam Chomsky

Noam Chomsky (1928 -) is a leading figure in philosophy and linguistics, and has been described as the 'father of modern linguistics'. He is also a political activist and describes himself as a 'libertarian socialist'. He is a radical thinker on public issues and a challenger of unjust power and delusions.

If we don't believe in freedom of expression for people we despise, we don't believe in it at all.

Propaganda is to a democracy what the bludgeon is to a totalitarian state.

 The more you can increase fear of drugs and crime, welfare mothers, immigrants and aliens, the more you control all the people.

Everyone's worried about stopping terrorism. Well, there's really an easy way: Stop participating in it.

Either you repeat the same conventional doctrines everybody is saying, or else you say something true, and it will sound like it's from Neptune.

The Bible is one of the most genocidal books in history.

The intellectual tradition is one of servility to power, and if I didn't betray it I'd be ashamed of myself.

As soon as questions of will or decision or reason or choice of action arise, human science is at a loss.

Colorless green ideas sleep furiously.

#29b
In this possibly terminal phase of human existence, democracy and freedom are more than just ideals to be valued - they may be essential to survival.

#29
We shouldn't be looking for heroes, we should be looking for good ideas.

The whole educational and professional training system is a very elaborate filter, which just weeds out people who are too independent, and who think for themselves, and who don't know how to be submissive, and so on -- because they're dysfunctional to the institutions.

The smart way to keep people passive and obedient is to strictly limit the spectrum of acceptable opinion, but allow very lively debate within that spectrum.

All over the place, from the popular culture to the propaganda system, there is constant pressure to make people feel that they are helpless, that the only role they can have is to ratify decisions and to consume.

I was never aware of any other option but to question everything.

Education is a system of imposed ignorance.

How it is we have so much information, but know so little?

Discovery is the ability to be puzzled by simple things.

For the powerful, crimes are those that others commit.

#30
That's the whole point of good propaganda. You want to create a slogan that nobody's going to be against, and everybody's going to be for. Nobody knows what it means, because it doesn't mean anything. WAR ON.... •

23

Neoliberal democracy; instead of citizens, it produces consumers. Instead of communities, it produces shopping malls. The net result is an atomized society of disengaged individuals who feel demoralized and socially powerless.

Science is a bit like the joke about the drunk who is looking under a lamppost for a key that he has lost on the other side of the street, because that's where the light is. It has no other choice.

WALT DISNEY

Walt Disney (1901 – 66) was a pioneer of the animation industry. His first popular success was the development of Mickey Mouse in 1928. From this he became increasingly ambitious and created several classic film length animations, and developed animated and live action films. He developed these themes further in the 1950s with the opening of the amusement park Disneyland.

If you can dream it, you can do it.

All our dreams can come true, if we have the courage to pursue them.

Somehow, I can't believe that there are any heights that can't be scaled by a man who knows the secret of making dreams come true.

We keep moving forward, opening new doors, and doing new things, because we're curious and curiosity keeps leading us down new paths.

It's kind of fun to do the impossible.

I would rather entertain and hope that people learned something than educate people and hope they were entertained.

The way to get started is to quit talking and begin doing.

Once a man has tasted freedom, he will never be content to be a slave.

I only hope that we never lose sight of one thing — that it was all started by a mouse.

You may not realize it when it happens, but a kick in the teeth may be the best thing in the world for you.

The more you like yourself, the less you are like anyone else, which makes you unique.

The era we are living in today is a dream of coming true.

Girls bored me, they still do. I love Mickey Mouse more than any woman I've ever known

When you're curious, you find lots of interesting things to do.

A person should set his goals as early as he can and devote all his energy and talent to getting there. With enough effort, he may achieve it. Or he may find something that is even more rewarding. But in the end, no matter what the outcome, he will know he has been alive.

When you believe in a thing, believe in it all the way, implicitly and unquestionable.

Over at our place, we're sure of just one thing: everybody in the world was once a child.

I suppose my formula might be: dream, diversify and never miss an angle.

We're not trying to entertain the critics ... I'll take my chances with the public.

Courage is the main quality of leadership, in my opinion, no matter where it is exercised.

Laughter is timeless. Imagination has no age. And dreams are forever.

Too many people grow up. That's the real trouble with the world, too many people grow up. They don't remember what it's like to be 12 years old. They patronize, they treat children as inferiors. Well I won't do that.

FREDERICK DOUGLAS

Frederick Douglas (c1818 – 1895) was the most influential African American of the 19th century. He was a social reformer, writer and statesman. He escaped from slavery and became a leading abolitionist noted for his oratory and the strength of his writing. He wrote supporting many liberal issues including women's rights, free public education and the abolition of capital punishment.

The white man's happiness cannot be purchased by the black man's misery.

Right is of no sex, Truth is of no color, God is the Father of us all, and we are all Brethren.

Knowledge unfits a child to be a slave

It is easier to build strong children than to repair broken men.

The soul that is within me no man can degrade.

One and God make a majority.

Intelligence is a great leveler here as elsewhere

No man can put a chain about the ankle of his fellow man without at last finding the other end fastened about his own neck.

Though conscious of the difficulty of learning without a teacher, I set out with high hope, and a fixed purpose, at whatever cost of trouble, to learn how to read.

The ground which a colored man occupies in this country is, every inch of it, sternly disputed.

I will, in the name of humanity which is outraged, in the name of liberty which is fettered, in the name of the constitution and the Bible, which are disregarded and trampled upon, dare to call in question and to denounce, with all the emphasis I can command, everything that serves to perpetuate slavery

For it is not light that is needed, but fire; it is not the gentle shower, but thunder. We need the storm, the whirlwind, and the earthquake. The feeling of the nation must be quickened; the conscience of the nation must be roused; the propriety of the nation must be startled; the hypocrisy of the nation must be exposed; and its crimes against God and man must be proclaimed and denounced.

Those who profess to favor freedom, and yet depreciate agitation, are men who want crops without plowing up the ground.

Power concedes nothing without a demand. It never did and it never will.

The Constitution itself. Its language is 'we the people'. Not we the white people, not even we the citizens, not we the privileged class, not we the high, not we the low, but we the people.

Opportunity is important but exertion is indispensable.

If nothing is expected of a people, that people will find it difficult to contradict that expectation.

Though they come as the waves come, we shall be all the stronger if we receive them as friends and give them a reason for loving our country and our institutions.

All great qualities are never found in any one man or in any one race. The whole of humanity, like the whole of everything else, is ever greater than a part. Men only know themselves by knowing others, and contact is essential to this knowledge.

No man can be truly free whose liberty is dependent upon the thought, feeling and action of others, and who has himself no means in his own hands for guarding, protecting, defending and maintaining that liberty.

If the negro knows enough to fight for his country he knows enough to vote; if he knows enough to pay taxes for the support of the government, he knows enough to vote; if he knows as much when sober, as an Irishman knows when drunk, he knows enough to vote.

BOB DYLAN

Bob Dylan (1941 -) is a singer songwriter whose musical style grew from folk and blues music which he expanded to give it a greater intellectualism and ambition. His most famous work was created during the early to mid-sixties during a period of great social unrest and change in America and across the wider world.

No one is free, even the birds are chained to the sky

Take care of all your memories. For you cannot relive them

He not busy being born is busy dying.

What's money? A man is a success if he gets up in the morning and goes to bed at night and in between does what he wants to do.

Behind every beautiful thing, there's some kind of pain.

I accept chaos, I'm not sure whether it accepts me.

Don't criticize what you can't understand.

Sometimes it's not enough to know what things mean, sometimes you have to know what things don't mean.

I think women rule the world and that no man has ever done anything that a woman either hasn't allowed him to do or encouraged him to do.

Some people feel the rain. Others just get wet.

All the money you make will never buy back your soul.

Charity is supposed to cover up for a multitude of sins.

Every pleasures got an edge of pain, pay for your ticket and don't complain.

People don't do what they believe in, they just do what's most convenient, then they repent.

When you got nothing, you got nothing to lose.

Feel ashamed to live in a land where justice is a game.

Ah, but I was so much older then, I'm younger than that now.

 I think of a hero as someone who understands the degree of responsibility that comes with his freedom.

Sailin' 'round the world in a dirty gondola,

Oh, to be back in the land of Coca-Cola!

Well the future for me is already a thing of the past.

All this talk about equality. The only thing people really have in common is that they are all going to die.

AMELIA EARHART

Amelia Earhart (1897 – 1937) was a pioneer aviator and the first women to fly solo across the Atlantic Ocean. She set many records and was also a bestselling author recounting her experiences providing inspiration to future generations of female aviators. In 1937 in an attempt to circumnavigate the world she disappeared over the Pacific Ocean.

After midnight, the moon set, and I was alone with the stars. I have often said that the lure of flying is the lure of beauty, and I need no other flight to convince me that the reason flyers fly, whether they know it or not, is the esthetic appeal of flying.

Courage is the price that life exacts for granting peace.

The most effective way to do it, is to do it.

Anticipation, I suppose, sometimes exceeds realization.

The most difficult thing is the decision to act. The rest is merely tenacity.

Adventure is worthwhile in itself.

A single act of kindness throws out roots in all directions, and the roots spring up and make new trees. CRUELTY

Don't criticize someone doing something you said couldn't be done

Preparation, I have often said, is rightly two-thirds of any venture

Everyone has oceans to fly, if they have the heart to do it. Is it reckless? Maybe – but what do dreams know of boundaries?

There's more to life than being a passenger.

Women will gain economic justice by proving themselves in all lines of endeavor, not by having laws passed for them.

Unfortunately, I lived at a time when girls were still girls. Though reading was considered proper, many of my outdoor exercises were not.

Probably no scientific development is more startling than the effect of this new and growing economic independence upon women themselves.

THOMAS EDISON

Thomas Edison (1847 – 1931) was a prolific inventor and businessman. He eventually held over 1,000 US patents as well as patents in many other countries. His invention of the electrical light, motion pictures and the recording of sound has had a profound effect on modern life.

Our greatest weakness lies in giving up. The most certain way to succeed is always to try just one more time.

Just because something doesn't do what you planned it to do doesn't mean it's useless.

There is no substitute for hard work.

I have not failed. I've just found 10,000 ways that won't work.

If we did all the things we are capable of, we would literally astound ourselves.

What you are will show in what you do.

Opportunity is missed by most people because it is dressed in overalls and looks like work.

The three great essentials to achieve anything worthwhile are: Hard work, Stick-to-itiveness, and Common sense.

Maturity is often more absurd than youth and very frequently is most unjust to youth.

Genius is one percent inspiration and ninety-nine percent perspiration.

I never did a day's work in my life. It was all fun.

Being busy does not always mean real work. The object of all work is production or accomplishment and to either of these ends there must be forethought, system, planning, intelligence, and honest purpose, as well as perspiration. Seeming to do is not doing.

I have friends in overalls whose friendship I would not swap for the favor of the kings of the world.

Everything comes to him who hustles while he waits.

I never did anything by accident, nor did any of my inventions come by accident; they came by work.

Nearly every man who develops an idea works it up to the point where it looks impossible, and then he gets discouraged. That's not the place to become discouraged.

To invent, you need a good imagination and a pile of junk.

Hell, there are no rules here - we're trying to accomplish something.

Waste is worse than loss. The time is coming when every person who lays claim to ability will keep the question of waste before him constantly. The scope of thrift is limitless.

Restlessness is discontent and discontent is the first necessity of progress. Show me a thoroughly satisfied man and I will show you a failure.

Be courageous. I have seen many depressions in business. Always America has emerged from these stronger and more prosperous. Be brave as your fathers before you. Have faith! Go forward!

The chief function of the body is to carry the brain around.

Many of life's failures are people who did not realize how close they were to success when they gave up.

There's a way to do it better - find it.

Your worth consists in what you are and not in what you have.

There will, one day, spring from the brain of science a machine or force so fearful in its potentialities, so absolutely terrifying, that even man, the fighter, who will dare torture and death in order to inflict torture and death, will be appalled, and so abandon war forever.

The best thinking has been done in solitude. The worst has been done in turmoil.

To have a great idea, have a lot of them.

The value of an idea lies in the using of it.

Results! Why, man, I have gotten a lot of results. I know several thousand things that won't work.

One might think that the money value of an invention constitutes its reward to the man who loves his work. But... I continue to find my greatest pleasure, and so my reward, in the work that precedes what the world calls success.

There is far more opportunity than there is ability.

Anything that won't sell, I don't want to invent. Its sale is proof of utility, and utility is success.

When I have fully decided that a result is worth getting I go ahead of it and make trial after trial until it comes.

I start where the last man left off.

Great ideas originate in the muscles.

Our schools are not teaching students to think. It is astonishing how many young people have difficulty in putting their brains definitely and systematically to work

The doctor of the future will give no medicine, but will interest his patients in the care of the human body, in diet, and in the cause and prevention of disease.

ALBERT EINSTEIN

Albert Einstein (1879 - 1955) was a pre-eminent theoretical physicist. His work on the general theory of relativity represented a step change in the understanding of how the universe worked, much of this work being done while working as a technical assistant at a Swiss patent office.

You can't blame gravity for falling in love.

Insanity: doing the same thing over and over again and expecting different results.

Look deep into nature, and then you will understand everything better.

Learn from yesterday, live for today, hope for tomorrow. The important thing is not to stop questioning.

Try not to become a man of success, but rather try to become a man of value.

When you are courting a nice girl an hour seems like a second. When you sit on a red-hot cinder a second seems like an hour. That's relativity.

The true sign of intelligence is not knowledge but imagination.

We cannot solve our problems with the same thinking we used when we created them.

To raise new questions, new possibilities, to regard old problems from a new angle, requires creative imagination and marks real advance in science.

The world is a dangerous place to live; not because of the people who are evil, but because of the people who don't do anything about it

It has become appallingly obvious that our technology has exceeded our humanity.

Education is what remains after one has forgotten what one has learned in school.

Only two things are infinite, the universe and human stupidity, and I'm not sure about the former.

Once we accept our limits, we go beyond them.

The only source of knowledge is experience.

Anyone who has never made a mistake has never tried anything new.

Life is like riding a bicycle. To keep your balance, you must keep moving.

Logic will get you from A to B. Imagination will take you everywhere.

It is the supreme art of the teacher to awaken joy in creative expression and knowledge.

I have no special talent. I am only passionately curious.

Everyone should be respected as an individual, but no one idolized.

A man should look for what is, and not for what he thinks should be.

Few are those who see with their own eyes and feel with their own hearts

Do not worry about your difficulties in mathematics. I can assure you mine are still greater.

Peace cannot be kept by force; it can only be achieved by understanding.

Weakness of attitude becomes weakness of character.

It is a miracle that curiosity survives formal education.

Whoever is careless with the truth in small matters cannot be trusted with important matters.

I do not believe that civilization will be wiped out in a war fought with the atomic bomb. Perhaps two-thirds of the people of the earth will be killed.

If you can't explain it simply, you don't understand it well enough.

Our task must be to free ourselves by widening our circle of compassion to embrace all living creatures and the whole of nature and its beauty.

All that is valuable in human society depends upon the opportunity for development accorded the individual.

Pure mathematics is, in its way, the poetry of logical ideas.

Reading, after a certain age, diverts the mind too much from its creative pursuits. Any man who reads too much and uses his own brain too little falls into lazy habits of thinking.

Science without religion is lame, religion without science is blind.

Everything should be made as simple as possible, but not simpler.

The monotony and solitude of a quiet life stimulates the creative mind.

41

If we knew what it was we were doing, it would not be called research, would it?

Imagination is more important than knowledge.

It's not that I'm so smart, it's just that I stay with problems longer.

Knowledge of what is does not open the door directly to what should be.

Reality is merely an illusion, albeit a very persistent one.

It stands to the everlasting credit of science that by acting on the human mind it has overcome man's insecurity before himself and before nature.

The important thing is not to stop questioning. Curiosity has its own reason for existing.

Common sense is the collection of prejudices acquired by age eighteen.

Nothing is more destructive of respect for the government and the law of the land than passing laws which cannot be enforced.

Sometimes one pays most for the things one gets for nothing.

In order to be an immaculate member of a flock of sheep, one must above all be a sheep oneself.

We still do not know one thousandth of one percent of what nature has revealed to us.

I never think of the future - it comes soon enough.

Imagination is everything. It is the preview of life's coming attractions.

The value of a man should be seen in what he gives and not in what he is able to receive.

If you are out to describe the truth, leave elegance to the tailor.

There comes a time when the mind takes a higher plane of knowledge but can never prove how it got there.

It is only to the individual that a soul is given.

My religion consists of a humble admiration of the illimitable superior spirit who reveals himself in the slight details we are able to perceive with our frail and feeble mind.

Great spirits have always encountered violent opposition from mediocre minds.

It gives me great pleasure indeed to see the stubbornness of an incorrigible nonconformist warmly acclaimed.

A table, a chair, a bowl of fruit and a violin; what else does a man need to be happy?

We shall require a substantially new manner of thinking if mankind is to survive.

The environment is everything that isn't me.

There are two ways to live: you can live as if nothing is a miracle; you can live as if everything is a miracle.

Concern for man and his fate must always form the chief interest of all technical endeavors. Never forget this in the midst of your diagrams and equations. — FACEBOOK

The devil has put a penalty on all things we enjoy in life. Either we suffer in health or we suffer in soul or we get fat.

I want to know all Gods thoughts; all the rest are just details.

43

The distinction between the past, present and future is only a stubbornly persistent illusion.

One strength of the communist system of the East is that it has some of the character of a religion and inspires the emotions of a religion.

The pursuit of truth and beauty is a sphere of activity in which we are permitted to remain children all our lives.

Too many of us look upon Americans as dollar chasers. This is a cruel libel, even if it is reiterated thoughtlessly by the Americans themselves.

I very rarely think in words at all. A thought comes, and I may try to express it in words afterwards.

It was the experience of mystery - even if mixed with fear - that engendered religion.

It should be possible to explain the laws of physics to a barmaid.

Human beings must have action; and they will make it if they cannot find it.

The unleashed power of the atom has changed everything save our modes of thinking and we thus drift toward unparalleled catastrophe

Never do anything against conscience even if the state demands it.

There could be no fairer destiny for any physical theory than that it should point the way to a more comprehensive theory in which it lives on as a limiting case.

The whole of science is nothing more than a refinement of everyday thinking.

Any man who can drive safely while kissing a pretty girl is simply not giving the kiss the attention it deserves.

You ask me if I keep a notebook to record my great ideas. I've only ever had one.

Coincidence is God's way of remaining anonymous.

Intellectual growth should commence at birth and cease only at death.

Without deep reflection one knows from daily life that one exists for other people.

Most people say that it is the intellect which makes a great scientist. They are wrong: it is character.

Few people are capable of expressing with equanimity opinions which differ from the prejudices of their social environment. Most people are even incapable of forming such opinions.

All religions, arts and sciences are branches of the same tree.

I know not with what weapons World War III will be fought, but World War IV will be fought with sticks and stones.

The only reason for time is so that everything doesn't happen at once.

The gift of fantasy has meant more to me than my talent for absorbing positive knowledge.

True religion is real living; living with all one's soul, with all one's goodness and righteousness.

RICHARD FEYNMAN

Richard Feynman (1918 – 88) was a theoretical physicist who jointly won the 1965 Nobel Prize for his work on quantum electrodynamics. He helped with the development of the atomic bomb in WW2 and developed the idea of nanotechnology.

Nobody ever figures out what life is all about, and it doesn't matter. Explore the world. Nearly everything is really interesting if you go into it deeply enough.

Study hard what interests you the most in the most undisciplined, irreverent and original manner possible.

Physics is like sex: sure, it may give some practical results, but that's not why we do it.

You have no responsibility to live up to what other people think you ought to accomplish. I have no responsibility to be like they expect me to be. It's their mistake, not my failing.

I learned very early the difference between knowing the name of something and knowing something.

I... a universe of atoms, an atom in the universe.

The first principle is that you must not fool yourself and you are the easiest person to fool.

The highest forms of understanding we can achieve are laughter and human compassion.

Religion is a culture of faith; science is a culture of doubt.

Physics isn't the most important thing. Love is.

I think it's much more interesting to live not knowing than to have answers which might be wrong.

If you thought that science was certain - well, that is just an error on your part.

All the time you're saying to yourself, 'I could do that, but I won't,' — which is just another way of saying that you can't.

There are 10^11 stars in the galaxy. That used to be a huge number. But it's only a hundred billion. It's less than the national deficit! We used to call them astronomical numbers. Now we should call them economical numbers.

For a successful technology, reality must take precedence over public relations, for nature cannot be fooled.

Philosophy of science is about as useful to scientists as ornithology is to birds.

I would rather have questions that can't be answered than answers that can't be questioned.

Nature uses only the longest threads to weave her patterns, so each small piece of her fabric reveals the organization of the entire tapestry.

As usual, nature's imagination far surpasses our own, as we have seen from the other theories which are subtle and deep.

Astronomy is older than physics. In fact, it got physics started by showing the beautiful simplicity of the motion of the stars and planets, the understanding of which was the beginning of physics. But the most remarkable discovery in all of astronomy is that the stars are made of atoms of the same kind as those on the earth.

But the real glory of science is that we can find a way of thinking such that the law is evident.

Einstein was a giant. His head was in the clouds, but his feet were on the ground. Those of us who are not so tall have to choose.

I believe that a scientist looking at nonscientific problems is just as dumb as the next guy.

There is a computer disease that anybody who works with computers knows about. It's a very serious disease and it interferes completely with the work. The trouble with computers is that you 'play' with them.

To those who do not know mathematics it is difficult to get across a real feeling as to the beauty, the deepest beauty, of nature. If you want to learn about nature, to appreciate nature, it is necessary to understand the language that she speaks in.

When I found out that Santa Claus wasn't real, I wasn't upset; rather, I was relieved that there was a much simpler phenomenon to explain how so many children all over the world got presents on the same night! The story had been getting pretty complicated -- it was getting out of hand.

Our imagination is stretched to the utmost, not, as in fiction, to imagine things which are not really there, but just to comprehend those things which are there.

But I don't have to know an answer. I don't feel frightened by not knowing things, by being lost in a mysterious universe within any purpose, which is the way it really is, so far as I can tell. It doesn't frighten me.

I'd hate to die twice. It's so boring.

HENRY FORD

Henry Ford (1863 – 1947) was an American industrialist and founded the Ford Motor Company. His use of the assembly line as a method of production for his motor cars slashed their costs and opened ownership up to the middle classes. His most famous car was the Model T which sold for $825 in 1908.

Vision without execution is just hallucination.

Education is preeminently a matter of quality, not amount

There is one rule for the industrialist and that is: make the best quality goods possible at the lowest cost possible, paying the highest wages possible.

Whether you think you can, or you think you can't – you're right.

Employers only handle the money – it is the customer who pays the wages.

Quality means doing it right when no one is looking.

Thinking is the hardest work there is, which is probably the reason so few engage in it.

The only real mistake is the one from which we learn nothing.

If I had asked people what they wanted, they would have said 'faster horses.'

There are no big problems; there are just a lot of little problems.

You can't build a reputation on what you are going to do.

If there is any one secret of success, it lies in the ability to get the other person's point of view and see things from that person's angle as well as from your own.

Enthusiasm is the yeast that makes your hopes shine to the stars.

Any customer can have a car painted any colour that he wants so long as it is black.

The gifted man bears his gifts into the world, not for his own benefit, but for the people among whom he is placed; for the gifts are not his, he himself is a gift to the community.

Of all the follies the elder generation falls victim to this is the most foolish, namely, the constant criticism of the younger element who will not be and cannot be like ourselves because we and they are different tribes produced of different elements in the great spirit of Time.

The most dangerous notion a young man can acquire is that there is no more room for originality. There is no large room for anything else.

Little difficulties are made to swell until they fill our horizon while the real big blessings of life are dwindled down to nothing.

Every success is the mother of countless others.

Individualism is what makes cooperation worth living.

History is more or less bunk.

Wars are necessary to teach us lessons we seem unable to learn any other way.

There is no such thing as no chance.

BENJAMIN FRANKLIN

Benjamin Franklin (1706 -90) was a polymath and one of the Founding Fathers of the United States of America having signed the declaration of independence. His contribution went far beyond this though being a scientist, politician, author, diplomat and an inventor.

Anyone who trades liberty for security deserves neither liberty nor security.

He that is good for making excuses is seldom good for anything else.

To lengthen thy life, lessen thy meals.

Without continual growth and progress, such words as improvement, achievement, and success have no meaning.

I didn't fail the test, I just found 100 ways to do it wrong.

He that displays too often his wife and his wallet is in danger of having both of them borrowed.

To Follow by faith alone is to follow blindly.

We are all born ignorant, but one must work hard to remain stupid.

If a man empties his purse into his head, no man can take it away from him. An investment in knowledge always pays the best interest.

Speak ill of no man, but speak all the good you know of everybody.

Energy and persistence conquer all things.

To succeed, jump as quickly at opportunities as you do at conclusions.

Trickery and treachery are the practices of fools that have not the wits enough to be honest.

The Constitution only gives people the right to pursue happiness. You have to catch it yourself.

It takes many good deeds to build a good reputation, and only one bad one to lose it.

 Being ignorant is not so much a shame, as being unwilling to learn.

Do not fear mistakes. You will know failure. Continue to reach out.

Any fool can criticize, condemn and complain and most fools do.

When you're finished changing, you're finished.

How few there are who have courage enough to own their faults, or resolution enough to mend them.

Write your injuries in dust, your benefits in marble.

Anger is never without a reason, but seldom with a good one.

A small leak can sink a great ship.

By failing to prepare, you are preparing to fail.

He that speaks much, is much mistaken.

The way to see by Faith is to shut the Eye of Reason.

In this world nothing is certain but death and taxes.

The worst wheel of the cart makes the most noise.

Tell me and I forget. Teach me and I remember. Involve me and I learn.

Do good to your friends to keep them, to your enemies to win them.

To be humble to superiors is duty, to equals courtesy, to inferiors nobleness.

Wine is constant proof that God loves us and loves to see us happy.

He that would live in peace and at ease must not speak all he knows, nor judge all he sees.

The greatest monarch on the proudest throne is obliged to sit upon his own arse.

Little strokes fell great oaks.

Lost time is never found again.

He that has once done you a kindness will be more ready to do you another, than he whom you yourself have obliged.

Resolve to perform what you ought; perform without fail what you resolve.

To find out a girl's faults, praise her to her girl friends.

Money never made a man happy yet, nor will it. The more a man has, the more he wants. Instead of filling a vacuum, it makes one.

Sin is not hurtful because it is forbidden, but it is forbidden because it is hurtful.

Without Freedom of thought, there can be no such Thing as Wisdom; and no such thing as public Liberty, without Freedom of speech.

Three may keep a secret, if two of them are dead.

The best thing to give to your enemy is forgiveness; to an opponent, tolerance; to a friend, your heart; to your child, a good example; to a father, deference; to your mother, conduct that will make her proud of you; to yourself, respect; to all men, charity.

Be studious in your profession, and you will be learned. Be industrious and frugal, and you will be rich. Be sober and temperate, and you will be healthy. Be in general virtuous, and you will be happy. At least you will, by such conduct, stand the be.

Originality is the art of concealing your sources.

MILTON FRIEDMAN

Milton Friedman (1912 – 2006) was the foremost economist of his time and received the Nobel Prize for Economics in 1974. His major contribution came in the field of monetary economics advocating what became known as monetarism which was widely adopted by central banks. He was a leading champion and popularizer of free markets.

If you put the federal government in charge of the Sahara Desert, in 5 years there'd be a shortage of sand.

A society that puts equality before freedom will get neither. A society that puts freedom before equality will get a high degree of both.

Underlying most arguments against the free market is a lack of belief in freedom itself.

Nothing is so permanent as a temporary government program.

Governments never learn. Only people learn.

There's no such thing as a free lunch.

Hell hath no fury like a bureaucrat scorned.

The government solution to a problem is usually as bad as the problem.

Concentrated power is not rendered harmless by the good intentions of those who create it.

Many people want the government to protect the consumer. A much more urgent problem is to protect the consumer from the government.

I am favor of cutting taxes under any circumstances and for any excuse, for any reason, whenever it's possible.

There is no place for government to prohibit consumers from buying products the effect of which will be to harm themselves.

With some notable exceptions, businessmen favor free enterprise in general but are opposed to it when it comes to themselves.

The society that puts equality before freedom will end up with neither. The society that puts freedom before equality will end up with a great measure of both.

The great virtue of a free market system is that it does not care what color people are; it does not care what their religion is; it only cares whether they can produce something you want to buy. It is the most effective system we have discovered to enable people who hate one another to deal with one another and help one another.

Thanks to economists, all of us, from the days of Adam Smith and before right down to the present, tariffs are perhaps one tenth of one percent lower than they otherwise would have been. ... And because of our efforts, we have earned our salaries ten-thousand fold.

I'm in favor of legalizing drugs. According to my values system, if people want to kill themselves, they have every right to do so. Most of the harm that comes from drugs is because they are illegal.

To the free man, the country is the collection of individuals who compose it, not something over and above them.

Only a crisis—actual or perceived—produces real change. When that crisis occurs, the actions that are taken depend on the ideas that are lying around.

History suggests only that capitalism is a necessary condition for political freedom. Clearly it is not a sufficient condition.

A major source of objection to a free economy is precisely that it ... gives people what they want instead of what a particular group thinks they ought to want. Underlying most arguments against the free market is a lack of belief in freedom itself.

The key insight of Adam Smith's Wealth of Nations is misleadingly simple: if an exchange between two parties is voluntary, it will not take place unless both believe they will benefit from it. Most economic fallacies derive from the neglect of this simple insight, from the tendency to assume that there is a fixed pie that one party can gain only at the expense of another.

The proper role of government is to prevent other people from harming an individual.

When everybody owns something, nobody owns it, and nobody has a direct interest in maintaining or improving its condition. That is why buildings in the Soviet Union—like public housing in the United States—look decrepit within a year or two of their construction.

Inflation is taxation without legislation.

ROBERT FROST

Robert Frost (1874 – 1963) was a leading poet and one of those rare 'public literary figures, almost a public institution'. He was the winner of four Pulitzer Prizes for his poetry and a special guest at President Kennedy's inauguration. He was a modern poet often on dark themes with an adherence to language as it is actually spoken.

Forgive, O Lord, my little jokes on Thee
And I'll forgive Thy great big one on me.

How many things would you attempt
If you knew you could not fail

In three words I can sum up everything I've learned about life: it goes on.

These woods are lovely, dark and deep, But I have promises to keep, And miles to go before I sleep, And miles to go before I sleep.

Two roads diverged in a wood, and I-- I took the one less traveled by, And that has made all the difference.

The best way out is always through.

Love is an irresistible desire to be irresistibly desired.

Education is the ability to listen to almost anything without losing your temper or your self-confidence.

Freedom lies in being bold.

Home is the place where, when you have to go there, they have to take you in.

Don't ever take a fence down until you know why it was put up.

No tears in the writer, no tears in the reader. No surprise in the writer, no surprise in the reader.

A poem begins as a lump in the throat, a sense of wrong, a homesickness, a lovesickness.

Half the world is composed of people who have something to say and can't, and the other half who have nothing to say and keep on saying it.

Happiness makes up in height for what it lacks in length.

To be a poet is a condition, not a profession.

Poetry is when an emotion has found its thought and the thought has found words.

There is one thing more exasperating than a wife who can cook and won't, and that's a wife who can't cook and will.

A jury consists of twelve persons chosen to decide who has the better lawyer.

Thinking is not to agree or disagree. That's voting.

Ends and beginnings—there are no such things.
There are only middles.

A poem begins in delight and ends in wisdom.

The best things and the best people rise out of their separateness;
I'm against a homogenized society because I want the cream to rise.

Most of the change we think we see in life is due to truths being in and out of favor.

Take care to sell your horse before he dies. The art of life is passing losses on.

There are two kinds of teachers: the kind that fill you with so much quail shot that you can't move, and the kind that just gives you a little prod behind and you jump to the skies.

A liberal is a man too broad minded to take his own side in a quarrel.

JOHN KENNETH GALBRAITH

John Kenneth Galbraith (1908 – 2006) was a leading economist and public intellectual. He was different to other leading economists in that he didn't produce grandiose theoretical support for his ideas, but did represent the view as to skepticism of markets and the importance of the role of the state. These views he popularized with many successful books.

Politics is not the art of the possible. It consists in choosing between the disastrous and the unpalatable.

Faced with the choice between changing one's mind and proving that there is no need to do so, almost everyone gets busy on the proof.

Economists are economical, among other things, of ideas; most make those of their graduate days last a lifetime.

The modern conservative is engaged in one of man's oldest exercises in moral philosophy; that is, the search for a superior moral justification for selfishness.

We all agree that pessimism is a mark of superior intellect.

The enemy of the conventional wisdom is not ideas but the march of events.

War remains the decisive human failure.

All successful revolutions are the kicking in of a rotten door.

It has been the acknowledged right of every Marxist scholar to read into Marx the particular meaning that he himself prefers and to treat all others with indignation.

61

In economics, hope and faith coexist with great scientific pretension and also a deep desire for respectability.

Do not be alarmed by simplification, complexity is often a device for claiming sophistication, or for evading simple truths.

In any great organization it is far, far safer to be wrong with the majority than to be right alone.

People who are in a fortunate position always attribute virtue to what makes them so happy.

When you see reference to a new paradigm you should always, under all circumstances, take cover.

It is a far, far better thing to have a firm anchor in nonsense than to put out on the troubled seas of thought.

The greater the wealth the thicker will be the dirt.

Power is as power does.

A nuclear war does not defend a country and it does not defend a system. I've put it the same way many times; not even the most accomplished ideologue will be able to tell the difference between the ashes of capitalism and the ashes of communism.

If all else fails, immortality can always be assured by spectacular error.

Meetings are indispensable when you don't want to do anything.

The happiest time of anyone's life is just after the first divorce.

Where humor is concerned there are no standards - no one can say what is good or bad, although you can be sure that everyone will.

All of the great leaders have had one characteristic in common: it was the willingness to confront unequivocally the major anxiety of their people in their time. This, and not much else, is the essence of leadership.

Money is a singular thing. It ranks with love as man's greatest source of joy. And with death as his greatest source of anxiety. Over all history it has oppressed nearly all people in one of two ways: either it has been abundant and very unreliable, or reliable and very scarce.

One of the greatest pieces of economic wisdom is to know what you do not know.

The conventional view serves to protect us from the painful job of thinking.

BILL GATES

Bill Gates (1955 -) is a leading businessman, having co-founded Microsoft, an inventor and a philanthropist. He is one of the pioneers of the computer age and the personal computer revolution. Since he stepped down as CEO of Microsoft he has made large donations to charitable organizations and to research and plans to donate 95% of his wealth to charities.

Information technology and business are becoming inextricably interwoven. I don't think anybody can talk meaningfully about one without the talking about the other.

Life is not fair; get used to it.

If you give people tools, and they use their natural ability and their curiosity, they will develop things in ways that will surprise you very much beyond what you might have expected.

Be nice to nerds. Chances are you'll end up working for one.

Technology is just a tool. In terms of getting the kids working together and motivating them, the teacher is the most important.

As we look ahead into the next century, leaders will be those who empower others.

If you can't make it good, at least make it look good.

If you think your teacher is tough, wait until you get a boss. He doesn't have tenure.

Success is a lousy teacher. It seduces smart people into thinking they can't lose.

I'm a great believer that any tool that enhances communication has profound effects in terms of how people can learn from each other, and how they can achieve the kind of freedoms that they're interested in.

#56 We always overestimate the change that will occur in the next two years and underestimate the change that will occur in the next ten. Don't let yourself be lulled into inaction.

#57 To create a new standard it takes something that's not just a little bit different. It takes something that's really new and really captures people's imagination. And the Macintosh, of all the machines I've ever seen, is the only one that meets that standard.

Your most unhappy customers are your greatest source of learning.

Great organizations demand a high level of commitment by the people involved.

Just in terms of allocation of time resources, religion is not very efficient. There's a lot more I could be doing on a Sunday morning.

Life is not divided into semesters. You don't get summers off and very few employers are interested in helping you find yourself.

It's fine to celebrate success but it is more important to heed the lessons of failure.

If GM had kept up with technology like the computer industry has, we would all be driving $25 cars that got 1000 MPG.

Our success has really been based on partnerships from the very beginning.

I really had a lot of dreams when I was a kid, and I think a great deal of that grew out of the fact that I had a chance to read a lot.

Every day we were saying, 'How can we keep this customer happy?' How can we get ahead in innovation by doing this, because if we don't, somebody else will.

This is a fantastic time to be entering the business world, because business is going to change more in the next 10 years than it has in the last 50.

The vision is really about empowering workers, giving them all the information about what's going on so they can do a lot more than they've done in the past.

The Internet is becoming the town square for the global village of tomorrow.

Television is not real life. In real life people actually have to leave the coffee shop and go to jobs.

Governments will always play a huge part in solving big problems. They set public policy and are uniquely able to provide the resources to make sure solutions reach everyone who needs them. They also fund basic research, which is a crucial component of the innovation that improves life for everyone

Discrimination has a lot of layers that make it tough for minorities to get a leg up.

You have to have a certain realism that government is a pretty blunt instrument, and without the constant attention of highly qualified people with the right metrics, it will fall into not doing things very well.

Should there be cameras everywhere in outdoor streets? My personal view is having cameras in inner cities is a very good thing. In the case of London, petty crime has gone down. They catch terrorists because of it. And if something really bad happens, most of the time you can figure out who did it.

What's amazing is, if young people understood how doing well in school makes the rest of their life so much more interesting, they would be more motivated. It's so far away in time that they can't appreciate what it means for their whole life.

Treatment without prevention is simply unsustainable.

Headlines, in a way, are what mislead you because bad news is a headline, and gradual improvement is not.

Corruption is one of the most common reasons I hear in views that criticize aid.

You may have heard of Black Friday and Cyber Monday. There's another day you might want to know about: Giving Tuesday. The idea is pretty straightforward. On the Tuesday after Thanksgiving, shoppers take a break from their gift-buying and donate what they can to charity.

Driving up the value of the advertising is a big commitment for Microsoft.

Research shows that there is only half as much variation in student achievement between schools as there is among classrooms in the same school. If you want your child to get the best education possible, it is actually more important to get him assigned to a great teacher than to a great school.

I was lucky to be involved and get to contribute to something that was important, which is empowering people with software.

At Microsoft there are lots of brilliant ideas but the image is that they all come from the top - I'm afraid that's not quite right.

By 2018, an estimated 63 percent of all new U.S. jobs will require workers with an education beyond high school. For our young people to get those jobs, they first need to graduate from high school ready to start a postsecondary education.

If I'd had some set idea of a finish line, don't you think I would have crossed it years ago?

By the time we see that climate change is really bad, your ability to fix it is extremely limited... The carbon gets up there, but the heating effect is delayed. And then the effect of that heat on the species and ecosystem is delayed. That means that even when you turn virtuous, things are actually going to get worse for quite a while.

Nuclear energy, in terms of an overall safety record, is better than other energy.

We make the future sustainable when we invest in the poor, not when we insist on their suffering.

The malaria parasite has been killing children and sapping the strength of whole populations for tens of thousands of years. It is impossible to calculate the harm malaria has done to the world.

The U.S. immigration laws are bad - really, really bad. I'd say treatment of immigrants is one of the greatest injustices done in our government's name.

Eradications are special. Zero is a magic number. You either do what it takes to get to zero and you're glad you did it; or you get close, give up and it goes back to where it was before, in which case you wasted all that credibility, activity, money that could have been applied to other things.

If you're a person struggling to eat and stay healthy, you might have heard about Michael Jordan or Muhammad Ali, but you'll never have heard of Bill Gates.

For Africa to move forward, you've really got to get rid of malaria.

The nuclear approach I'm involved in is called a traveling-wave reactor, which uses waste uranium for fuel. There's a lot of things

that have to go right for that dream to come true - many decades
building demo plants, proving the economics are right. But if it
does, you could have cheaper energy with no CO2 emissions

.

ULYSSES S GRANT

Ulysses S Grant (1822- 95) was the victorious commanding general of the American Army during the American Civil war, working closely with Abraham Lincoln. He subsequently became the 18th President of the United States. His presidency was overshadowed by the corruption charges against his cabinet members during his first term, and the economic recession in his second term.

The art of war is simple enough. Find out where your enemy is. Get at him as soon as you can. Strike him as hard as you can, and keep moving on.

I don't know why black skin may not cover a true heart as well as a white one.

I know only two tunes: one of them is 'Yankee Doodle', and the other one isn't.

The war is over — the rebels are our countrymen again.

Although a soldier by profession, I have never felt any sort of fondness for war, and I have never advocated it, except as a means of peace.

As the United States is the freest of all nations, so, too, its people sympathize with all people struggling for liberty and self-government; but while so sympathizing it is due to our honor that we should abstain from enforcing our views upon unwilling nations and from taking an interested part, without invitation,

I have never advocated war except as a means of peace.

We felt that it was a stain to the Union that men should be bought and sold like cattle.

Labor disgraces no man; unfortunately, you occasionally find men who disgrace labor.

If men make war in slavish obedience to rules, they will fail.

I know no method to secure the repeal of bad or obnoxious laws so effective as their stringent execution.

The will of the people is the best law.

Cheap cigars come in handy: they stifle the odor of cheap politicians.

Garfield has shown that he is not possessed of the backbone of an angle-worm.

No other terms than unconditional and immediate surrender. I propose to move immediately upon your works.

In every battle there comes a time when both sides consider themselves beaten, then he who continues the attack wins.

There never was a time when, in my opinion, some way could not be found to prevent the drawing of the sword.

I never wanted to get out of a place as much as I did to get out of the presidency.

There are but few important events in the affairs of men brought about by their own choice.

ERNEST HEMMINGWAY

Ernest Hemmingway (1899 – 1961) was one of the great American novelists and won the Nobel Prize for Literature in 1954. His understated writing style influenced many writers and his adventurous lifestyle captured the public imagination. He committed suicide in 1961.

The world breaks everyone, and afterward, some are strong at the broken places.

They wrote in the old days that it is sweet and fitting to die for one's country. But in modern war, there is nothing sweet nor fitting in your dying. You will die like a dog for no good reason.

There is no friend as loyal as a book.

There is nothing to writing. All you do is sit down at a typewriter and bleed.

I drink to make other people more interesting.

Every day is a new day. It is better to be lucky. But I would rather be exact. Then when luck comes you are ready.

Never think that war, no matter how necessary, nor how justified, is not a crime.

Every man's life ends the same way. It is only the details of how he lived and how he died that distinguish one man from another.

I can't stand it to think my life is going so fast and I'm not really living it.

No, that is the great fallacy: the wisdom of old men. They do not grow wise. They grow careful.

Today is only one day in all the days that will ever be. But what happen in all the other days that ever come can depend on what you do today.

The first panacea for a mismanaged nation is inflation of the currency; the second is war. Both bring a temporary prosperity; both bring a permanent ruin. But both are the refuge of political and economic opportunists.

You know what makes a good loser? Practice.

God knows, people who are paid to have attitudes toward things, professional critics, make me sick; camp-following eunuchs of literature.

Life isn't hard to manage when you've nothing to lose.

There is no lonelier man in death, except the suicide, than that man who has lived many years with a good wife and then outlived her. If two people love each other there can be no happy end to it.

Critics are men who watch a battle from a high place then come down and shoot the survivors.

They say the seeds of what we will do are in all of us, but it always seemed to me that in those who make jokes in life the seeds are covered with better soil and with a higher grade of manure.

Before you react, think. Before you spend, earn. Before you criticize, wait. Before you quit, try.

Never confuse movement with action.

There are only three sports: bullfighting, motor racing, and mountaineering; all the rest are merely games.

Courage is grace under pressure.

It is good to have an end to journey toward; but it is the journey that matters, in the end

EDWIN HUBBLE

Edwin Hubble (1889 - 1953) was a leading astronomer who advanced the understanding of galaxies beyond our own. His development of 'red shift' combined with his observations showed that the universe was expanding, and logically started from a single point in the 'Big Bang'. His achievements were honored with the naming of the 'Hubble Space Telescope'.

Past time is finite, future time is infinite.

All nature is a vast symbolism: Every material fact has sheathed within it a spiritual truth

The history of astronomy is a history of receding horizons.

Not until the empirical resources are exhausted, need we pass on to the dreamy realms of speculation.

Observation always involves theory.

Science is the one human activity that is truly progressive. The body of positive knowledge is transmitted from generation to generation.

Equipped with his five senses, man explores the universe around him and calls the adventure Science.

Eventually, we reach the utmost limits of our telescopes. There, we measure shadows and search among ghostly errors of measurement for landmarks that are scarcely more substantial.

We do not know why we are born into the world, but we can try to find out what sort of a world it is — at least in its physical aspects

We find them smaller and fainter, in constantly increasing numbers, and we know that we are reaching into space, farther and farther, until, with the faintest nebulae that can be detected with the greatest telescopes, we arrive at the frontier of the known universe.

The whole thing is so much bigger than I am, and I can't understand it, so I just trust myself to it; and forget about it.

I chucked the law for astronomy, and I knew that even if I were second-rate or third-rate, it was astronomy that mattered.

Wisdom cannot be directly transmitted, and does not readily accumulate through the ages.

Positive, objective knowledge is public property. It can be transmitted directly from one person to another, it can be pooled, and it can be passed on from one generation to the next. Consequently, knowledge accumulates through the ages, each generation adding its contribution.

The scientist explores the world of phenomena by successive approximations. He knows that his data are not precise and that his theories must always be tested. It is quite natural that he tends to develop healthy skepticism, suspended judgment, and disciplined imagination.

THOMAS JEFFERSON

Thomas Jefferson (1743 -1826) was a Founding Father of the United States of America and the main author of the Declaration of Independence. He was the second elected vice president, under John Adams. and served as the third president of the United States.

Do you want to know who you are? Don't ask. Act! Action will delineate and define you.

I predict future happiness for Americans, if they can prevent the government from wasting the labors of the people under the pretense of taking care of them.

Honesty is the first chapter of the book wisdom.

The legitimate powers of government extend to such acts only as are injurious to others. It does me no injury for my neighbor to say there are twenty gods or no god. It neither picks my pocket nor breaks my leg.

I sincerely believe that banking establishments are more dangerous than standing armies, and that the principle of spending money to be paid by posterity, under the name of funding, is but swindling futurity on a large scale.

The most valuable of all talents is that of never using two words when one will do.

I'm a greater believer in luck, and I find the harder I work the more I have of it.

The man who reads nothing at all is better educated than the man who reads nothing but newspapers.

On matters of style, swim with the current, on matters of principle, stands like a rock.

We in America do not have government by the majority. We have government by the majority who participate.

Our civil rights have no dependence on our religious opinions any more than our opinions in physics or geometry.

Nothing gives one person so much advantage over another as to remain always cool and unruffled under all circumstances.

If a nation expects to be ignorant and free, in a state of civilization, it expects what never was and never will be.

I have no fear that the result of our experiment will be that men may be trusted to govern themselves without a master.

Experience hath shewn, that even under the best forms (of government) those entrusted with power have, in time, and by slow operations, perverted it into tyranny.

Be polite to all, but intimate with few.

We hold these truths to be self-evident: that all men are created equal; that they are endowed by their Creator with certain inalienable rights; that among these are life, liberty, and the pursuit of happiness.

He who knows best knows how little he knows.

Whenever the people are well-informed, they can be trusted with their own government.

To penetrate and dissipate these clouds of darkness, the general mind must be strengthened by education.

On the dogmas of religion, as distinguished from moral principles, all mankind, from the beginning of the world to this day, have been quarreling, fighting, burning and torturing one another, for abstractions unintelligible to themselves and to all others, and absolutely beyond the comprehension of the human mind.

Power is not alluring to pure minds.

When angry, count ten before you speak; if very angry, an hundred.

Never spend your money before you have earned it.

The glow of one warm thought is to me worth more than money.

The moment a person forms a theory, his imagination sees in every object only the traits which favor that theory.

He, who receives ideas from me, receives instruction himself without lessening mine; as he who lights his taper at mine receives light without darkening me.

I have seen enough of one war never to wish to see another.

I never will, by any word or act, bow to the shrine of intolerance or admit a right of inquiry into the religious opinions of others.

Leave all the afternoon for exercise and recreation, which are as necessary as reading. I will rather say more necessary because health is worth more than learning.

STEVE JOBS

Steve Jobs (1955 – 2011) was an entrepreneur and inventor who co- founded Apple and was the CEO and majority shareholder. He was a pioneer of the computer revolution of the 1970s and 80s and built Apple into the largest company in the world.

Your work is going to fill a large part of your life, and the only way to be truly satisfied is to do what you believe is great work. And the only way to do great work is to love what you do. If you haven't found it yet, keep looking. Don't settle. As with all matters of the heart, you'll know when you find it.

Your time is limited, so don't waste it living someone else's life. Don't be trapped by dogma - which is living with the results of other people's thinking. Don't let the noise of others' opinions drown out your own inner voice. And most important, have the courage to follow your heart and intuition.

Be a yardstick of quality. Some people aren't used to an environment where excellence is expected.

No one wants to die. Even people who want to go to heaven don't want to die to get there. And yet death is the destination we all share. No one has ever escaped it. And that is as it should be, because Death is very likely the single best invention of Life. It is Life's change agent. It clears out the old to make way for the new.

Great things in business are never done by one person. They're done by a team of people.

Everyone here has the sense that right now is one of those moments when we are influencing the future.

Innovation distinguishes between a leader and a follower.

My favorite things in life don't cost any money. It's really clear that the most precious resource we all have is time.

For the past 33 years, I have looked in the mirror every morning and asked myself: 'If today were the last day of my life, would I want to do what I am about to do today?' And whenever the answer has been 'No' for too many days in a row, I know I need to change something.

Remembering that you are going to die is the best way I know to avoid the trap of thinking you have something to lose. You are already naked. There is no reason not to follow your heart.

Being the richest man in the cemetery doesn't matter to me. Going to bed at night saying we've done something wonderful, that's what matters to me.

And no, we don't know where it will lead. We just know there's something much bigger than any of us here.

It is piracy, not overt online music stores, which is our main competitor.

I'm an optimist in the sense that I believe humans are noble and honorable, and some of them are really smart. I have a very optimistic view of individuals.

But innovation comes from people meeting up in the hallways or calling each other at 10:30 at night with a new idea, or because they realized something that shoots holes in how we've been thinking about a problem.

Throughout my years in business, I discovered something. I would always ask why you do things. The answers that I would invariably get are: 'Oh, that's just the way things are done around here.' Nobody knows why they do what they do. Nobody thinks very deeply about things in business.

As individuals, people are inherently good. I have a somewhat more pessimistic view of people in groups. And I remain extremely concerned when I see what's happening in our country, which is in many ways the luckiest place in the world. We don't seem to be excited about making our country a better place for our kids.

I'm sorry, it's true. Having children really changes your view on these things. We're born, we live for a brief instant, and we die. It's been happening for a long time. Technology is not changing it much - if at all.

Our goal is to make the best devices in the world, not to be the biggest.

If you haven't found it yet, keep looking. Don't settle. As with all matters of the heart, you'll know when you find it. And, like any great relationship, it just gets better and better as the years roll on.

I believe life is an intelligent thing: that things aren't random.

Bottom line is, I didn't return to Apple to make a fortune. I've been very lucky in my life and already have one. When I was 25, my net worth was $100 million or so. I decided then that I wasn't going to let it ruin my life. There's no way you could ever spend it all, and I don't view wealth as something that validates my intelligence.

When you're young, you look at television and think, there's a conspiracy. The networks have conspired to dumb us down. But when you get a little older, you realize that's not true. The networks are in business to give people exactly what they want.

Our DNA is as a consumer company - for that individual customer who's voting thumbs up or thumbs down. That's who we think about. And we think that our job is to take responsibility for the complete user experience. And if it's not up to par, it's our fault, plain and simply.

That's been one of my mantras — focus and simplicity. Simple can be harder than complex; you have to work hard to get your thinking clean to make it simple.

I think if you do something and it turns out pretty good, then you should go do something else wonderful, not dwell on it for too long. Just figure out what's next.

When you're a carpenter making a beautiful chest of drawers, you're not going to use a piece of plywood on the back, even though it faces the wall and nobody will see it. You'll know it's there, so you're going to use a beautiful piece of wood on the back. For you to sleep well at night, the aesthetic, the quality, has to be carried all the way through.

Creativity is just connecting things. When you ask creative people how they did something, they feel a little guilty because they didn't really do it, they just saw something. It seemed obvious to them after a while.

Here's to the crazy ones, the misfits, the rebels, the troublemakers, the round pegs in the square holes... The ones who see things differently — they're not fond of rules... You can quote them, disagree with them, glorify or vilify them, but the only thing you can't do is ignore them because they change things... They push the human race forward, and while some may see them as the crazy ones, we see genius, because the ones who are crazy enough to think that they can change the world, are the ones who do.

It's better to be a pirate than to join the navy.

Stay hungry. Stay foolish.

Ultimately, it comes down to taste. It comes down to trying to expose yourself to the best things that humans have done and then try to bring those things into what you're doing. Picasso had a saying: good artists copy, great artists steal. And we have always been shameless about stealing great ideas, and I think part of what made the Macintosh great was that the people working on it were musicians and poets and artists and zoologists and historians who also happened to be the best computer scientists in the world.

MICHAEL JORDAN

Michael Jordan (1963 -) is a retired basketball player and commonly considered to have been the greatest player of all time. He was also responsible for the increasing popularity of the NBA in the 1980s – 90s.

Why pay a dollar for a bookmark? Why not use the dollar for a bookmark?

If you're trying to achieve, there will be roadblocks. I've had them; everybody has had them. But obstacles don't have to stop you. If you run into a wall, don't turn around and give up. Figure out how to climb it, go through it, or work around it.

My attitude is that if you push me towards something that you think is a weakness, then I will turn that perceived weakness into a strength.

Talent wins games, but teamwork and intelligence wins championships.

Just play. Have fun. Enjoy the game.

I can accept failure, everyone fails at something. But I can't accept not trying.

I've missed more than 9000 shots in my career. I've lost almost 300 games. 26 times, I've been trusted to take the game winning shot and missed. I've failed over and over and over again in my life. And that is why I succeed.

Some people want it to happen, some wish it would happen, others make it happen.

Always turn a negative situation into a positive situation.

I hope the millions of people I've touched have the optimism and desire to share their goals and hard work and persevere with a positive attitude.

Be true to the game, because the game will be true to you. If you try to shortcut the game, then the game will shortcut you. If you put forth the effort, good things will be bestowed upon you. That's truly about the game, and in some ways that's about life too.

Sometimes, things may not go your way, but the effort should be there every single night.

When I lose the sense of motivation and the sense to prove something as a basketball player, it's time for me to move away from the game.

I play to win, whether during practice or a real game. And I will not let anything get in the way of me and my competitive enthusiasm to win.

To be successful you have to be selfish, or else you never achieve. And once you get to your highest level, then you have to be unselfish. Stay reachable. Stay in touch. Don't isolate.

In college I never realized the opportunities available to a pro athlete. I've been given the chance to meet all kinds of people, to travel and expand my financial capabilities, to get ideas and learn about life, to create a world apart from basketball.

I'm not out there sweating for three hours every day just to find out what it feels like to sweat.

It's a heavy duty to try to do everything and please everybody. My job was to go out there and play the game of basketball as best I can and provide entertainment for everyone who wanted to watch basketball. Obviously, people may not agree with that; again, I can't live with what everyone's impression of what I should or what I shouldn't do.

You have to expect things of yourself before you can do them.

I think the players win the championship, and the organization has something to do with it, don't get me wrong. But don't try to put the organization above the players.

My heroes are and were my parents. I can't see having anyone else as my heroes.

Sometimes you need to get hit in the head to realize that you're in a fight.

The game has its ups and downs, but you can never lose focus of your individual goals and you can't let yourself be beat because of lack of effort.

How many times have your parents told you not to do things, and the next thing you know, you go do it? And you realized you shouldn't have done it.

Obstacles don't have to stop you. If you run into a wall, don't turn around and give up. Figure out how to climb it, go through it, or work around it.

My body could stand the crutches but my mind couldn't stand the sideline.

I never looked at the consequences of missing a big shot . . . when you think about the consequences you always think of a negative result.

I know fear is an obstacle for some people, but it is an illusion to me . . . Failure always made me try harder next time.

If you accept the expectations of others, especially negative ones, then you never will change the outcome.

I realize that I'm black, but I like to be viewed as a person, and this is everybody's wish.

But my drive to win is so great ... I just step over that line. ... It's very embarrassing, ... one of the things you totally regret. So you look at yourself in the mirror and say, 'I was stupid.

HELEN KELLER

Helen Keller (1880 – 1968) was born with the ability to see and hear. However, at 19 months she contracted a serious illness that left her both blind and deaf. The story of her education and her teacher, Anne Sullivan, is told in the film 'The Miracle Worker'. Helen Keller went on to become a world famous author and speaker and a powerful advocate for people with disabilities, women's rights and pacifism.

Life is either a great adventure or nothing.

The best and most beautiful things in the world cannot be seen or even touched - they must be felt with the heart.

Although the world is full of suffering, it is also full of the overcoming of it.

When one door of happiness closes, another opens; but often we look so long at the closed door that we do not see the one which has been opened for us.

Keep your face to the sunshine and you cannot see a shadow.

Optimism is the faith that leads to achievement. Nothing can be done without hope and confidence.

Alone we can do so little; together we can do so much.

I long to accomplish a great and noble task, but it is my chief duty to accomplish small tasks as if they were great and noble.

The highest result of education is tolerance.

No pessimist ever discovered the secret of the stars, or sailed to an uncharted land, or opened a new doorway for the human spirit.

Character cannot be developed in ease and quiet. Only through experience of trial and suffering can the soul be strengthened, ambition inspired, and success achieved.

Smell is a potent wizard that transports you across thousands of miles and all the years you have lived.

I would rather walk with a friend in the dark, than alone in the light.

Death is no more than passing from one room into another. But there's a difference for me, you know. Because in that other room I shall be able to see.

What we once enjoyed and deeply loved we can never lose, for all that we love deeply becomes a part of us.

People don't like to think, if one thinks, one must reach conclusions. Conclusions are not always pleasant.

A bend in the road is not the end of the road...Unless you fail to make the turn.

I do not want the peace which passeth understanding, I want the understanding which bringeth peace.

The bulk of the world's knowledge is an imaginary construction.

Blindness cuts us off from things, but deafness cuts us off from people.

No matter how dull, or how mean, or how wise a man is, he feels that happiness is his indisputable right.

Believe. No pessimist ever discovered the secrets of the stars, or sailed to an uncharted land, or opened a new heaven to the human spirit.

It is for us to pray not for tasks equal to our powers, but for powers equal to our tasks, to go forward with a great desire forever beating at the door of our hearts as we travel toward our distant goal.

We would never learn to be brave and patient if there were only joy in the world.

JOHN F. KENNEDY

Jack Kennedy (1917 – 63) was the 35th President of the United States till his assassination in Dallas. He was President during a difficult period when the cold was at its height and culminated in the Cuban missile crisis. He is the only Roman Catholic president.

As we express our gratitude, we must never forget that the highest appreciation is not to utter words, but to live by them.

Change is the law of life. And those who look only to the past or present are certain to miss the future.

The cost of freedom is always high, but Americans have always paid it. And one path we shall never choose, and that is the path of surrender, or submission.

Let us not seek the Republican answer or the Democratic answer, but the right answer. Let us not seek to fix the blame for the past. Let us accept our own responsibility for the future.

My fellow Americans, ask not what your country can do for you, ask what you can do for your country.

Forgive your enemies, but never forget their names.

The best road to progress is freedom's road.

The ignorance of one voter in a democracy impairs the security of all.

Physical fitness is not only one of the most important keys to a healthy body, it is the basis of dynamic and creative intellectual activity.

SELF-LEADERSHIP

Leadership and learning are indispensable to each other.

If art is to nourish the roots of our culture, society must set the artist free to follow his vision wherever it takes him.

I look forward to a great future for America - a future in which our country will match its military strength with our moral restraint, its wealth with our wisdom, its power with our purpose.

The great enemy of the truth is very often not the lie, deliberate, contrived and dishonest, but the myth, persistent, persuasive and unrealistic.

We are tied to the ocean. And when we go back to the sea, whether it is to sail or to watch - we are going back from whence we came.

Let every nation know, whether it wishes us well or ill, that we shall pay any price, bear any burden, meet any hardship, support any friend, oppose any foe to assure the survival and the success of liberty.

Efforts and courage are not enough without purpose and direction.

The goal of education is the advancement of knowledge and the dissemination of truth.

Geography has made us neighbors. History has made us friends. Economics has made us partners, and necessity has made us allies. Those whom God has so joined together, let no man put asunder.

Man is still the most extraordinary computer of all.

A nation that is afraid to let its people judge the truth and falsehood in an open market is a nation that is afraid of its people.

Too often we... enjoy the comfort of opinion without the discomfort of thought.

93

History is a relentless master. It has no present, only the past rushing into the future. To try to hold fast is to be swept aside.

Conformity is the jailer of freedom and the enemy of growth.

Our problems are man-made; therefore, they may be solved by man. And man can be as big as he wants. No problem of human destiny is beyond human beings.

Let us never negotiate out of fear. But let us never fear to negotiate.

I don't think the intelligence reports are all that hot. Some days I get more out of the New York Times.

The world knows that America will never start a war. This generation of Americans has had enough of war and hate... we want to build a world of peace where the weak are secure and the strong are just.

I am not the Catholic candidate for President. I am the Democratic Party's candidate for President, who happens also to be a Catholic.

Sure it's a big job; but I don't know anyone who can do it better than I can.

Our progress as a nation can be no swifter than our progress in education. The human mind is our fundamental resource.

Mankind must put an end to war before war puts an end to mankind.

The very word 'secrecy' is repugnant in a free and open society; and we are as a people inherently and historically opposed to secret societies, to secret oaths, and to secret proceedings.

Victory has a thousand fathers, but defeat is an orphan.

Modern cynics and skeptics... see no harm in paying those to whom they entrust the minds of their children a smaller wage than is paid to those to whom they entrust the care of their plumbing.

The problems of the world cannot possibly be solved by skeptics or cynics whose horizons are limited by the obvious realities. We need men who can dream of things that never were.

War will exist until that distant day when the conscientious objector enjoys the same reputation and prestige that the warrior does today.

Mothers all want their sons to grow up to be president, but they don't want them to become politicians in the process.

The time to repair the roof is when the sun is shining.

Our growing softness, our increasing lack of physical fitness, is a menace to our security.

A young man who does not have what it takes to perform military service is not likely to have what it takes to make a living. Today's military rejects include tomorrow's hard-core unemployed.

When written in Chinese, the word 'crisis' is composed of two characters. One represents danger and the other represents opportunity.

All free men, wherever they may live, are citizens of Berlin. And therefore, as a free man, I take pride in the words 'Ich bin ein Berliner!'

Tolerance implies no lack of commitment to one's own beliefs. Rather it condemns the oppression or persecution of others.

A child miseducated is a child lost.

I just received the following wire from my generous Daddy; Dear Jack, Don't buy a single vote more than is necessary. I'll be damned if I'm going to pay for a landslide.

There are risks and costs to action. But they are far less than the long range risks of comfortable inaction.

Those who dare to fail miserably can achieve greatly.

For time and the world do not stand still. Change is the law of life. And those who look only to the past or the present are certain to miss the future.

There is always inequality in life. Some men are killed in a war and some men are wounded and some men never leave the country. Life is unfair.

A man may die, nations may rise and fall, but an idea lives on.

I'm always rather nervous about how you talk about women who are active in politics, whether they want to be talked about as women or as politicians.

The world is very different now. For man holds in his mortal hands the power to abolish all forms of human poverty, and all forms of human life.

In a time of domestic crisis, men of goodwill and generosity should be able to unite regardless of party or politics.

Once you say you're going to settle for second, that's what happens to you in life.

The greater our knowledge increases the more our ignorance unfolds.

We prefer world law in the age of self-determination to world war in the age of mass extermination.

We stand today on the edge of a new frontier - the frontier of the 1960's - a frontier of unknown opportunities and perils - a frontier of unfulfilled hopes and threats.

When we got into office, the thing that surprised me most was to find that things were just as bad as we'd been saying they were.

For in the final analysis, our most basic common link is that we all inhabit this small planet. We all breathe the same air. We all cherish our children's futures. And we are all mortal.

I hope that no American will waste his franchise and throw away his vote by voting either for me or against me solely on account of my religious affiliation. It is not relevant.

Domestic policy can only defeat us; foreign policy can kill us.

I think this is the most extraordinary collection of talent, of human knowledge, that has ever been gathered at the White House - with the possible exception of when Thomas Jefferson dined alone.

If anyone is crazy enough to want to kill a president of the United States, he can do it. All he must be prepared to do is give his life for the president's.

Now we have a problem in making our power credible, and Vietnam is the place.

Do you realize the responsibility I carry? I'm the only person standing between Richard Nixon and the White House.

Why should man's first flight to the moon be a matter of national competition? Why should the United States and the Soviet Union, in preparing for such expeditions, become involved in immense duplications of research, construction and expenditure?

If a free society cannot help the many who are poor, it cannot save the few who are rich.

No one has been barred on account of his race from fighting or dying for America, there are no white or colored signs on the foxholes or graveyards of battle.

Khrushchev reminds me of the tiger hunter who has picked a place on the wall to hang the tiger's skin long before he has caught the tiger. This tiger has other ideas.

My brother Bob doesn't want to be in government - he promised Dad he'd go straight.

A nation which has forgotten the quality of courage which in the past has been brought to public life is not as likely to insist upon or regard that quality in its chosen leaders today - and in fact we have forgotten.

We believe that if men have the talent to invent new machines that put men out of work, they have the talent to put those men back to work.

Let the word go forth from this time and place, to friend and foe alike, that the torch has been passed to a new generation of Americans - born in this century, tempered by war, disciplined by a hard and bitter peace.

It is an unfortunate fact that we can secure peace only by preparing for war.

In a very real sense, it will not be one man going to the moon it will be an entire nation. For all of us must work to put him there.

MARTIN LUTHER KING JR.

Martin Luther King Jr. (1929 – 68) was a Baptist minister and the leader of the African-American Civil Rights movement. He fought for civil rights and against poverty and the Vietnam War using nonviolent civil disobedience. He received the Nobel Peace Prize in 1964.

Life's most persistent and urgent question is, 'What are you doing for others?'

Darkness cannot drive out darkness; only light can do that. Hate cannot drive out hate; only love can do that.

In the End, we will remember not the words of our enemies, but the silence of our friends.

The function of education is to teach one to think intensively and to think critically. Intelligence plus character - that is the goal of true education.

Love is the only force capable of transforming an enemy into friend.

I have decided to stick with love. Hate is too great a burden to bear.

Faith is taking the first step even when you don't see the whole staircase.

Nothing in all the world is more dangerous than sincere ignorance and conscientious stupidity.

I refuse to accept the view that mankind is so tragically bound to the starless midnight of racism and war that the bright daybreak of peace and brotherhood can never become a reality... I believe that unarmed truth and unconditional love will have the final word.

99

The ultimate measure of a man is not where he stands in moments of comfort and convenience, but where he stands at times of challenge and controversy.

We must accept finite disappointment, but never lose infinite hope.

I have a dream that my four little children will one day live in a nation where they will not be judged by the color of their skin, but by the content of their character.

We must develop and maintain the capacity to forgive. He who is devoid of the power to forgive is devoid of the power to love. There is some good in the worst of us and some evil in the best of us. When we discover this, we are less prone to hate our enemies.

We must learn to live together as brothers or perish together as fools.

Human progress is neither automatic nor inevitable... Every step toward the goal of justice requires sacrifice, suffering, and struggle; the tireless exertions and passionate concern of dedicated individuals.

A genuine leader is not a searcher for consensus but a molder of consensus.

The ultimate tragedy is not the oppression and cruelty by the bad people but the silence over that by the good people.

We are not makers of history. We are made by history.

The time is always right to do what is right.

Every man must decide whether he will walk in the light of creative altruism or in the darkness of destructive selfishness.

Everything that we see is a shadow cast by that which we do not see.

Violence as a way of achieving racial justice is both impractical immoral. I am not unmindful of the fact that violence often brings about momentary results. Nations have frequently won their independence in battle. But in spite of temporary victories, violence never brings permanent peace.

Change does not roll in on the wheels of inevitability, but comes through continuous struggle. And so we must straighten our backs and work for our freedom. A man can't ride you unless your back is bent.

Human salvation lies in the hands of the creatively maladjusted.

Never forget that everything Hitler did in Germany was legal.

It may be true that the law cannot make a man love me, but it can keep him from lynching me, and I think that's pretty important.

Nonviolence is a powerful and just weapon. which cuts without wounding and ennobles the man who wields it. It is a sword that heals.

There comes a time when people get tired of being pushed out of the glittering sunlight of life's July and left standing amid the piercing chill of an alpine November.

At the center of non-violence stands the principle of love.

A nation or civilization that continues to produce soft-minded men purchases its own spiritual death on the installment plan.

An individual has not started living until he can rise above the narrow confines of his individualistic concerns to the broader concerns of all humanity.

To other countries, I may go as a tourist, but to India, I come as a pilgrim.

I have a dream that one day on the red hills of Georgia, the sons of former slaves and the sons of former slave owners will be able to sit together at the table of brotherhood.

The first question which the priest and the Levite asked was: 'If I stop to help this man, what will happen to me?' But... the good Samaritan reversed the question: 'If I do not stop to help this man, what will happen to him?'

If physical death is the price that I must pay to free my white brothers and sisters from a permanent death of the spirit, then nothing can be more redemptive.

The hottest place in Hell is reserved for those who remain neutral in times of great moral conflict.

Peace is not merely a distant goal that we seek, but a means by which we arrive at that goal.

Almost always, the creative dedicated minority has made the world better.

We who in engage in nonviolent direct action are not the creators of tension. We merely bring to the surface the hidden tension that is already alive.

Don't let anybody make you think God chose America as His divine messianic force to be a sort of policeman of the whole world.

Shallow understanding from people of good will is more frustrating than absolute misunderstanding from people of ill will.

The question is not whether we will be extremists, but what kind of extremists we will be... The nation and the world are in dire need of creative extremists.

Any religion that professes to be concerned about the souls of men and is not concerned about the slums that damn them, the economic conditions that strangle them and the social conditions that cripple them is a spiritually moribund religion awaiting burial.

Have we not come to such an impasse in the modern world that we must love our enemies - or else? The chain reaction of evil - hate begetting hate, wars producing more wars - must be broken, or else we shall be plunged into the dark abyss of annihilation.

History will have to record that the greatest tragedy of this period of social transition was not the strident clamor of the bad people, but the appalling silence of the good people.

I believe that unarmed truth and unconditional love will have the final word in reality. This is why right, temporarily defeated, is stronger than evil triumphant.

The quality, not the longevity, of one's life is what is important.

Never succumb to the temptation of bitterness.

I am not interested in power for power's sake, but I'm interested in power that is moral, that is right and that is good.

If we are to go forward, we must go back and rediscover those precious values - that all reality hinges on moral foundations and that all reality has spiritual control.

The moral arc of the universe bends at the elbow of justice.

Wars are poor chisels for carving out peaceful tomorrows.

He who passively accepts evil is as much involved in it as he who helps to perpetrate it. He who accepts evil without protesting against it is really cooperating with it.

Our scientific power has outrun our spiritual power. We have guided missiles and misguided men.

All progress is precarious, and the solution of one problem brings us face to face with another problem.

The art of acceptance is the art of making someone who has just done you a small favor wish that he might have done you a greater one.

We may have all come on different ships, but we're in the same boat now.

Freedom is never voluntarily given by the oppressor; it must be demanded by the oppressed.

When you are right you cannot be too radical; when you are wrong, you cannot be too conservative.

Means we use must be as pure as the ends we seek.

Whatever your life's work is, do it well. A man should do his job so well that the living, the dead, and the unborn could do it no better.

There can be no deep disappointment where there is not deep love.

There is nothing more tragic than to find an individual bogged down in the length of life, devoid of breadth.

Discrimination is a hellhound that gnaws at Negroes in every waking moment of their lives to remind them that the lie of their inferiority is accepted as truth in the society dominating them.

Pity may represent little more than the impersonal concern which prompts the mailing of a check, but true sympathy is the personal concern which demands the giving of one's soul.

Giving All labor that uplifts humanity has dignity and importance and should be undertaken with painstaking excellence.

Excellence That old law about 'an eye for an eye' leaves everybod_ blind. The time is always right to do the right thing.

Law and order exist for the purpose of establishing justice and when they fail in this purpose they become the dangerously structured dams that block the flow of social progress.

Science investigates; religion interprets. Science gives man knowledge which is power; religion gives man wisdom which is control.

I have a dream that one day every valley shall be exalted, every hill and mountain shall be made low, the rough places will be made straight and the glory of the Lord shall be revealed and all flesh shall see it together.

We must use time creatively.

The past is prophetic in that it asserts loudly that wars are poor chisels for carving out peaceful tomorrows.

Capitalism does not permit an even flow of economic resources. With this system, a small privileged few are rich beyond conscience, and almost all others are doomed to be poor at some level. That's the way the system works. And since we know that the system will not change the rules, we are going to have to change the system.

Philanthropy is commendable, but it must not cause the philanthropist to overlook the circumstances of economic injustice which make philanthropy necessary.

Every man lives in two realms: the internal and the external. The internal is that realm of spiritual ends expressed in art, literature, morals, and religion. The external is that complex of devices, techniques, mechanisms, and instrumentalities by means of which we live.

If a man has not discovered something that he will die for, he isn't fit to live.

Discovered the hope of a secure and livable world lies with disciplined nonconformists who are dedicated to justice, peace and brotherhood.

We must build dikes of courage to hold back the flood of fear.

I just want to do God's will. And he's allowed me to go to the mountain. And I've looked over, and I've seen the Promised Land. I may not get there with you, but I want you to know tonight that we as a people will get to the Promised Land.

I submit that an individual who breaks a law that conscience tells him is unjust, and who willingly accepts the penalty of imprisonment in order to arouse the conscience of the community over its injustice, is in reality expressing the highest respect for law.

Since being in India, I am more convinced than ever before that the method of nonviolent resistance is the most potent weapon available to oppressed people in their struggle for justice and human dignity.

India One of the greatest casualties of the war in Vietnam is the Great Society... shot down on the battlefield of Vietnam.

The sweltering summer of the Negro's legitimate discontent will not pass until there is an invigorating autumn of freedom and equality.

If I wish to compose or write or pray or preach well, I must be angry. Then all the blood in my veins is stirred, and my understanding is sharpened.

It is incontestable and deplorable that Negroes have committed crimes; but they are derivative crimes. They are born of the greater crimes of the white society.

The principle of self-defense, even involving weapons and bloodshed, has never been condemned, even by Gandhi.

Oppressed people cannot remain oppressed forever. The yearning for freedom eventually manifests itself.

The Negro needs the white man to free him from his fears. The white man needs the Negro to free him from his guilt.

ABRAHAM LINCOLN

Abraham Lincoln (1809 – 65) was the 16th President of the United States till his assassination in 1865. He was leader of the country during the most difficult period – the American Civil War. The result of the civil war was that slavery was abolished and the Union continued.

I am a success today because I had a friend who believed in me and I didn't have the heart to let him down.

If I had eight hours to chop down a tree, I'd spend six hours sharpening my axe.

These capitalists generally act harmoniously and in concert, to fleece the people.

I am not bound to win, but I am bound to be true. I am not bound to succeed, but I am bound to live by the light that I have. I must stand with anybody that stands right, and stand with him while he is right, and part with him when he goes wrong.

The time comes upon every public man when it is best for him to keep his lips closed.

The best way to get a bad law repealed is to enforce it strictly.

Things may come to those who wait...but only the things left by those who hustle.

If you look for the bad in people expecting to find it, you surely will.

I like to see a man proud of the place in which he lives. I like to see a man live so that his place will be proud of him.

The ballot is stronger than the bullet.

Be sure you put your feet in the right place, then stand firm.

America will never be destroyed from the outside. If we falter and lose our freedoms, it will be because we destroyed ourselves.

To stand in silence when they should be protesting makes cowards out of men.

Most folks are about as happy as they make their minds up to be.

I walk slowly, but I never walk backward.

Don't worry when you are not recognized, but strive to be worthy of recognition.

Better to remain silent and be thought a fool than to speak out and remove all doubt.

My great concern is not whether you have failed, but whether you are content with your failure.

Sir, my concern is not whether God is on our side; my greatest concern is to be on God's side, for God is always right.

A friend is one who has the same enemies as you have.

A woman is the only thing I am afraid of that I know will not hurt me.

God must love the common man, he made so many of them.

Republicans are for both the man and the dollar, but in case of conflict the man before the dollar.

That some achieve great success, is proof to all that others can achieve it as well.

Those who deny freedom to others deserve it not for themselves.

A house divided against itself cannot stand.

I do the very best I know how, the very best I can, and I mean to keep on doing so until the end.

When I do good, I feel good. When I do bad, I feel bad. That's my religion.

The way for a young man to rise is to improve himself in every way he can, never suspecting that anybody wishes to hinder him.

You can have anything you want - if you want it badly enough. You can be anything you want to be, do anything you set out to accomplish if you hold to that desire with singleness of purpose.

What has once happened, will invariably happen again, when the same circumstances which combined to produce it, shall again combine in the same way.

Always bear in mind that your own resolution to succeed is more important than any one thing.

Surely God would not have created such a being as man, with an ability to grasp the infinite, to exist only for a day! No, no, man was made for immortality.

When I am getting ready to reason with a man, I spend one-third of my time thinking about myself and what I am going to say and two-thirds about him and what he is going to say.

Sorrow comes to all...Perfect relief is not possible, except with time. You cannot now realize that you will ever feel better and yet you are sure to be happy again.

With the fearful strain that is on me night and day, if I did not laugh I should die.

Towering genius disdains a beaten path.

I do not think much of a man who is not wiser today than he was yesterday.

No man is good enough to govern another man without that other's consent.

Suspicions which may be unjust need not be stated.

Important principles may and must be inflexible.

Whenever I hear anyone arguing for slavery, I feel a strong impulse to see it tried on him personally.

If I were two faced, would I be wearing this one.

Tact is the ability to describe others as they see themselves.

I care not for a man's religion whose dog and cat are not the better for it.

The leading rule for the lawyer, as for the man of every other calling, is diligence. Leave nothing for to-morrow which can be done to-day.

Die when I may, I want it said by those who knew me best that I always plucked a thistle and planted a flower where I thought a flower would grow.

It is better only sometimes to be right than at all times wrong.

Let the people know the truth and the country is safe.

He has a right to criticize, who has a heart to help.

I have always found that mercy bears richer fruits than strict justice.

You cannot keep out of trouble by spending more than you earn.

Nearly all men can stand adversity, but if you want to test a man's character, give him power.

Books serve to show a man that those original thoughts of his aren't very new after all.

We the people are the rightful masters of both Congress and the courts, not to overthrow the Constitution but to overthrow the men who pervert the Constitution.

Character is like a tree and reputation like a shadow. The shadow is what we think of it; the tree is the real thing.

When I hear a man preach, I like to see him act as if he were fighting bees.

You cannot help men permanently by doing for them what they could do for themselves.

You cannot build character and courage by taking away man's initiative and independence.

You cannot strengthen the weak by weakening the strong.

Lonely men seek companionship. Lonely women sit at home and wait. They never meet.

I can make a General in five minutes but a good horse is hard to replace.

To ease another's heartache is to forget one's own.

My dream is of a place and a time where America will once again be seen as the last best hope of earth.

NORMAN MAILER

Norman Mailer (1923 – 2007) was a novelist, journalist and political activist. He won the Pulitzer Prize for The Executioner' Song, which combined journalism and fiction, and was about the execution of Gary Gilmore. He was a combative figure and has been described as 'a colossus of American culture and literature in the 1960s, 70s and 80s'.

Every moment of one's existence one is growing into more or retreating into less. One is always living a little more or dying a little bit.

Writing books is the closest men ever come to childbearing.

There was that law of life, so cruel and so just, that one must grow or else pay more for remaining the same.

Sentimentality is the emotional promiscuity of those who have no sentiment.

The function of socialism is to raise suffering to a higher level.

The natural role of twentieth-century man is anxiety.

Any war that requires the suspension of reason as a necessity for support is a bad war.

You don't know a woman until you've met her in court.

The mark of mediocrity is to look for precedent.

Hungry fighters win fights.

Love asks us that we be a little braver than is comfortable, a little more generous, a little more flexible. It means living on the edge more than we care to.

Reaching consensus in a group is often confused with finding the right answer.

The difference between writing a book and being on television is the difference between conceiving a child and having a baby made in a test tube.

We love those who can lead us to a place we will never reach without them.

We didn't win the Cold War; we were just a big bank that bankrupted a smaller bank because we had an arms race that wiped the Russians out.

Once a newspaper touches a story, the facts are lost forever, even to the protagonists.

A modern democracy is a tyranny whose borders are undefined; one discovers how far one can go only by traveling in a straight line until one is stopped.

I am not here only so that the blind might see, but to teach those who thought they could see that they are blind

The true religion of America has always been America.

Los Angeles is a constellation of plastic.

Television is coitus interruptus brought into aesthetics

Dying can't be all that difficult-up to now everyone has managed to do it.

The ultimate tendency of liberalism is vegetarianism.

There is nothing safe about sex. There never will be.

MARILYN MONROE

Marilyn Monroe (1926 – 62) was a film actress and model who became one of the most popular icons of the 20th Century. She has been the most enduring of sex symbols and her private life, and death, have been the subject of much speculation.

I'm selfish, impatient, and a little insecure. I make mistakes, I'm out of control, and at times hard to handle. But if you can't handle me at my worst, then you sure as hell don't deserve me at my best.

I am good, but not an angel. I do sin, but I am not the devil. I am just a small girl in a big world trying to find someone to love.

Imperfection is beauty, madness is genius and it's better to be absolutely ridiculous than absolutely boring.

Give a girl the right shoes, and she can conquer the world.

Success makes so many people hate you. I wish it wasn't that way. It would be wonderful to enjoy success without seeing envy in the eyes of those around you.

The nicest thing for me is sleep, then at least I can dream.

I have always had a talent for irritating women since I was fourteen.

A woman can't be alone. She needs a man. A man and a woman support and strengthen each other. She just can't do it by herself.

The real lover is the man who can thrill you just by touching your head or smiling into your eyes - or just by staring into space.

Dreaming about being an actress, is more exciting than being one.

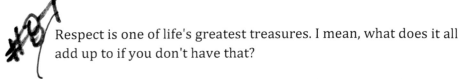

Respect is one of life's greatest treasures. I mean, what does it all add up to if you don't have that?

Girdles and wire stays should have never been invented. No man wants to hug a padded bird cage.

A woman can bring a new love to each man she loves, providing there are not too many.

My work is the only ground I've ever had to stand on. To put it bluntly, I seem to have a whole superstructure with no foundation, but I'm working on the foundation.

Having a child, that's always been my biggest fear. I want a child and I fear a child.

A man makes you feel important - makes you glad you are a woman.

It is wonderful to have someone praise you, to be desired.

Next to my husband, and along with Marlon Brando, I think that Yves Montand is the most attractive man I've ever met.

I guess I have always been deeply terrified to really be someone's wife since I know from life one cannot love another, ever, really.

I'll think I have a few wonderful friends and all of a sudden, ooh, here it comes. They do a lot of things. They talk about you to the press, to their friends, tell stories, and you know, it's disappointing.

Husbands are chiefly good as lovers when they are betraying their wives.

It's better to be unhappy alone than unhappy with someone - so far.

We are all of us stars, and we deserve to twinkle.

If a star or studio chief or any other great movie personages find themselves sitting among a lot of nobodies, they get frightened - as if somebody was trying to demote them.

A woman knows by intuition, or instinct, what is best for herself.

I've been on a calendar, but I've never been on time.

If I'd observed all the rules, I'd never have got anywhere.

Experts on romance say for a happy marriage there has to be more than a passionate love. For a lasting union, they insist, there must be a genuine liking for each other. Which, in my book, is a good definition for friendship.

Sometimes I've been to a party where no one spoke to me for a whole evening. The men, frightened by their wives or sweeties, would give me a wide berth. And the ladies would gang up in a corner to discuss my dangerous character.

I want to be an artist, not... a celluloid aphrodisiac.

Women who seek to be equal with men lack ambition.

I think one of the basic reasons men make good friends is that they can make up their minds quickly.

Sometimes I feel my whole life has been one big rejection.

I've often stood silent at a party for hours listening to my movie idols turn into dull and little people.

Consider the fellow. He never spends his time telling you about his previous night's date. You get the idea he has eyes only for you and wouldn't think of looking at another woman.

I don't know who invented high heels, but all women owe him a lot.

Hollywood is a place where they'll pay you a thousand dollars for a kiss and fifty cents for your soul.

Men are so willing to respect anything that bores them.

I am not a victim of emotional conflicts. I am human.

Naturally, there are times when every woman likes to be flattered... to feel she is the most important thing in someone's world. Only a man can paint this picture.

Designers want me to dress like Spring, in billowing things. I don't feel like Spring. I feel like a warm red Autumn.

Fame is fickle, and I know it. It has its compensations but it also has its drawbacks, and I've experienced them both.

I think that sexuality is only attractive when it's natural and spontaneous.

The trouble with censors is that they worry if a girl has cleavage. They ought to worry if she hasn't any.

There is just no comparison between having a dinner date with a man and staying home playing canasta with the girls.

Sometimes I think it would be easier to avoid old age, to die young, but then you'd never complete your life, would you? You'd never wholly know you.

I remember when I was in high school I didn't have a new dress for each special occasion. The girls would bring the fact to my attention, not always too delicately. The boys, however, never bothered with the subject. They were my friends, not because of the size of my wardrobe but because they liked me.

Of course, it does depend on the people, but sometimes I'm invited places to kind of brighten up a dinner table like a musician who'll play the piano after dinner, and I know you're not really invited for yourself. You're just an ornament.

No one ever told me I was pretty when I was a little girl. All little girls should be told they're pretty, even if they aren't.

One of the best things that ever happened to me is that I'm a woman. That is the way all females should feel.

I'm one of the world's most self-conscious people. I really have to struggle.

If your man is a sports enthusiast, you may have to resign yourself to his spouting off in a monotone on a prize fight, football game or pennant race.

All my stepchildren carried the burden of my fame. Sometimes they would read terrible things about me, and I'd worry about whether it would hurt them. I would tell them: 'Don't hide these things from me. I'd rather you ask me these things straight out, and I'll answer all your questions.'

I have feelings too. I am still human. All I want is to be loved, for myself and for my talent.

119

ROSA PARKS

Rosa Parks (1913 – 2005) was an activist for African American Civil Rights. Her most famous moment came in 1955 when she was sat in a 'colored section' of a bus and refused to give her seat up for a white passenger, and was arrested. She became a symbol of resistance to segregation.

Memories of our lives, of our works and our deeds will continue in others.

Racism is still with us. But it is up to us to prepare our children for what they have to meet, and, hopefully, we shall overcome.

People always say that I didn't give up my seat because I was tired, but that isn't true. I was not tired physically... No, the only tired I was, was tired of giving in.

I would like to be remembered as a person who wanted to be free... so other people would be also free.

I have learned over the years that when one's mind is made up, this diminishes fear; knowing what must be done does away with fear.

I'm tired of being treated like a second-class citizen.

Each person must live their life as a model for others.

Why do you all push us around?

All I was doing was trying to get home from work.

Have you ever been hurt and the place tries to heal a bit, and you just pull the scar off it over and over again.

Whatever my individual desires were to be free, I was not alone. There were many others who felt the same way.

At the time I was arrested I had no idea it would turn into this. It was just a day like any other day. The only thing that made it significant was that the masses of the people joined in.

I have been refused entrance on the buses because I would not pay my fare at the front and go around to the rear door to enter. That was the custom if the bus was crowded up to the point where the white passengers would start occupying.

I had felt for a long time that, if I was ever told to get up so a white person could sit, that I would refuse to do so.

God has always given me the strength to say what is right.

As far back as I can remember, I knew there was something wrong with our way of life when people could be mistreated because of the color of their skin.

Let us look at Jim Crow for the criminal he is and what he has done to one life multiplied millions of times over these United States and the world. He walks us on a tightrope from birth.

Whites would accuse you of causing trouble when all you were doing was acting like a normal human being instead of cringing.

The Rosa and Raymond Parks Institute accepts people of any race. We don't discriminate against anyone. We teach people to reach their highest potential. I set examples by the way I lead my life.

You spend your whole lifetime in your occupation, actually making life clever, easy and convenient for white people. But when you have to get transportation home, you are denied an equal accommodation. Our existence was for the white man's comfort and well-being; we had to accept being deprived of just being human.

I talked and talked of everything I know about the white man's inhuman treatment of the Negro.

In it not easy to remain rational and normal mentally in such a setting where, even in our airport in Montgomery, there is a white waiting room... There are restroom facilities for white ladies and colored women, white men and colored men. We stand outside after being served at the same ticket counter instead of sitting on the inside.

ELVIS PRESLEY

Elvis Presley (1935 – 77) was a rock musician who was known as 'The King of Rock and Roll'. He is one of the most famous icons of the 20th Century and was synonymous with the cultural revolution of the late 50s and 60s.

Rhythm is something you either have or don't have, but when you have it, you have it all over.

Truth is like the sun. You can shut it out for a time, but it ain't goin' away.

I'm not trying to be sexy. It's just my way of expressing myself when I move around.

They put me on television. And the whole thing broke loose. It was wild, I tell ya for sure.

Ambition is a dream with a V8 engine.

The Lord can give, and the Lord can take away. I might be herding sheep next year.

A live concert to me is exciting because of all the electricity that is generated in the crowd and on stage. It's my favorite part of the business, live concerts.

The image is one thing and the human being is another. It's very hard to live up to an image, put it that way.

People ask me where I got my singing style. I didn't copy my style from anybody.

Rock and roll music, if you like it, if you feel it, you can't help but move to it. That's what happens to me. I can't help it.

I think I have something tonight that's not quite correct for evening wear. Blue suede shoes

When I was a boy, I always saw myself as a hero in comic books and in movies. I grew up believing this dream.

I learned how important it is to entertain people and give them a reason to come and watch you play.

I'll never feel comfortable taking a strong drink, and I'll never feel easy smoking a cigarette. I just don't think those things are right for me.

I'm trying to keep a level head. You have to be careful out in the world. It's so easy to get turned.

I have no use for bodyguards, but I have very specific use for two highly trained certified public accountants.

Every time I think that I'm getting old, and gradually going to the grave, something else happens.

I don't think I'm bad for people. If I did think I was bad for people, I would go back to driving a truck, and I really mean this.

I've never written a song in my life. It's all a big hoax.

RONALD REAGAN

Ronald Reagan (1911 – 2004) started as a sports commentator after leaving college and progressed to become a Hollywood actor in several major films. He then became the 33rd Governor of California from 1967 – 75 and eventually became the 40th President of the United States of America from 1981 – 89. His legacy was a peaceful end to the cold war and a restoration of morale and pride in America.

I've noticed that everyone who is for abortion has already been born.

America is, and always will be, a shining city on a hill.

America is too great for small dreams.

Trees cause more pollution than automobiles do.

All the waste in a year from a nuclear power plant can be stored under a desk.

Socialism only works in two places: Heaven where they don't need it and hell where they already have it.

Information is the oxygen of the modern age. It seeps through the walls topped by barbed wire, it wafts across the electrified borders. ... The Goliath of totalitarianism will be brought down by the David of the microchip.

Recession is when your neighbor loses his job. Depression is when you lose yours. And recovery is when Jimmy Carter loses his.

You can't tax business. Business doesn't pay taxes. It collects taxes.

Unemployment insurance is a pre-paid vacation for freeloaders.

Welfare's purpose should be to eliminate, as far as possible, the need for its own existence.

Freedom is not free.

As government expands, liberty contracts.

Above all, we must realize that no arsenal, or no weapon in the arsenals of the world, is so formidable as the will and moral courage of free men and women.

A people free to choose will always choose peace.

The government is like a baby's alimentary canal, with a happy appetite at one end and no responsibility at the other.

The most terrifying words in the English language are: I'm from the government and I'm here to help.

Government's view of the economy could be summed up in a few short phrases: If it moves, tax it. If it keeps moving, regulate it. And if it stops moving, subsidize it.

Government is not a solution to our problem government is the problem.

Government's first duty is to protect the people, not run their lives.

If more government is the answer, then it was a really stupid question.

I know in my heart that man is good, that what is right will always eventually triumph, and there is purpose and worth to each and every life.

One way to make sure crime doesn't pay would be to let the government run it.

History teaches that war begins when governments believe the price of aggression is cheap.

Trust, but verify.

The greatest leader is not necessarily the one who does the greatest things. He is the one that gets the people to do the greatest things.

Radio was theater of the mind.

A picture is worth 1,000 denials.

We fought a war on poverty, and poverty won.

Now let's set the record straight. There's no argument over the choice between peace and war, but there's only one guaranteed way you can have peace—and you can have it in the next second—surrender.

JOHN D ROCKEFELLER

John D Rockefeller (1839 – 1937) was a tycoon of the oil industry who founded Standard oil. He started work as a relatively impecunious bookkeeper and finished life as the wealthiest man of modern times. He dedicated the last 40 years of his life to philanthropy and the creation of many charitable foundations.

I had no ambition to make a fortune. Mere money-making has never been my goal, I had an ambition to build.

The person who starts out simply with the idea of getting rich won't succeed; you must have a larger ambition. There is no mystery in business success. If you do each day's task successfully, and stay faithfully within these natural operations of commercial laws which I talk so much about, and keep your head clear, you will come out all right.

Charity is injurious unless it helps the recipient to become independent of it.

Singleness of purpose is one of the chief essentials for success in life, no matter what may be one's aim.

The ability to deal with people is as purchasable a commodity as sugar or coffee and I will pay more for that ability than for any other under the sun.

Every right implies a responsibility; every opportunity, an obligation, every possession, a duty.

I would rather earn 1% off a 100 people's efforts than 100% of my own efforts.

If your only goal is to become rich, you will never achieve it.

It is wrong to assume that men of immense wealth are always happy.

The road to happiness lies in two simple principles; find what interests you and that you can do well, and put your whole soul into it - every bit of energy and ambition and natural ability you have.

I believe in the dignity of labor, whether with head or hand; that the world owes no man a living but that it owes every man an opportunity to make a living.

Good management consists in showing average people how to do the work of superior people.

I know of nothing more despicable and pathetic than a man who devotes all the hours of the waking day to the making of money for money's sake.

I always tried to turn every disaster into an opportunity.

I do not think that there is any other quality so essential to success of any kind as the quality of perseverance. It overcomes almost everything, even nature.

I can think of nothing less pleasurable than a life devoted to pleasure.

If you want to succeed you should strike out on new paths, rather than travel the worn paths of accepted success.

I believe in the supreme worth of the individual and in his right to life, liberty, and the pursuit of happiness.

A friendship founded on business is better than a business founded on friendship.

Don't be afraid to give up the good to go for the great.

Next to doing the right thing, the most important thing is to let people know you are doing the right thing.

Do you know the only thing that gives me pleasure? It's to see my dividends coming in.

Don't blame the marketing department. The buck stops with the chief executive.

After it is all over, the religion of man is his most important possession.

And we are never too old to study the Bible. Each time the lessons are studied comes some new meaning, some new thought which will make us better.

I think it is a man's duty to make all the money he can, keep all that he can and give away all that he can.

The most important thing for a young man is to establish a credit, a reputation, character.

The way to make money is to buy when blood is running in the streets.

Having being endowed with the gift I possess, I believe it's my duty to make money and to use the money I make for the good of my fellow man according to the dictates of my conscience.

The secret of success is to do the common things uncommonly well.

ELEANOR ROOSEVELT

Eleanor Roosevelt (1884 -1962) was the longest serving First Lady serving during her husband's four terms as President. She changed the role of First Lady from being simply a hostess to one of political activism.

Great minds discuss ideas; average minds discuss events; small minds discuss people.

A woman is like a tea bag - you can't tell how strong she is until you put her in hot water.

You gain strength, courage, and confidence by every experience in which you really stop to look fear in the face. You are able to say to yourself, 'I lived through this horror. I can take the next thing that comes along.

You must do the things you think you cannot do.

The future belongs to those who believe in the beauty of their dreams.

One's philosophy is not best expressed in words; it is expressed in the choices one makes... and the choices we make are ultimately our responsibility.

Probably the happiest period in life most frequently is in middle age, when the eager passions of youth are cooled, and the infirmities of age not yet begun; as we see that the shadows, which are at morning and evening so large, almost entirely disappear at midday.

Happiness is not a goal; it is a by-product.

No one can make you feel inferior without your consent.

It isn't enough to talk about peace. One must believe in it. And it isn't enough to believe in it. One must work at it.

You can never really live anyone else's life, not even your child's. The influence you exert is through your own life, and what you've become yourself.

People grow through experience if they meet life honestly and courageously. This is how character is built.

Anyone who thinks must think of the next war as they would of suicide. We are afraid to care too much, for fear that the other person does not care at all.

There are practical little things in housekeeping which no man really understands.

I believe that anyone can conquer fear by doing the things he fears to do, provided he keeps doing them until he gets a record of successful experience behind him.

I cannot believe that war is the best solution. No one won the last war and no one will win the next war.

Do what you feel in your heart to be right- for you'll be criticized anyway. You'll be damned if you do, and damned if you don't.

I once had a rose named after me and I was very flattered. But I was not pleased to read the description in the catalogue: no good in a bed, but fine up against a wall.

The giving of love is an education in itself.

Since you get more joy out of giving joy to others, you should put a good deal of thought into the happiness that you are able to give.

The only advantage of not being too good a housekeeper is that your guests are so pleased to feel how very much better they are.

The battle for the individual rights of women is one of long standing and none of us should countenance anything which undermines it.

I think, at a child's birth, if a mother could ask a fairy godmother to endow it with the most useful gift, that gift should be curiosity.

It is not fair to ask of others what you are not willing to do yourself.

Never allow a person to tell you no, who doesn't have the power to say yes.

Anyone who knows history, particularly the history of Europe, will, I think, recognize that the domination of education or of government by any one particular religious faith is never a happy arrangement for the people.

Friendship with one's self is all important, because without it one cannot be friends with anyone else in the world.

If life were predictable it would cease to be life, and be without flavor.

Remember always that you not only have the right to be an individual, you have an obligation to be one.

Freedom makes a huge requirement of every human being. With freedom comes responsibility. For the person who is unwilling to grow up, the person who does not want to carry his own weight, this is a frightening prospect.

Too often the great decisions are originated and given form in bodies made up wholly of men, or so completely dominated by them that whatever of special value women have to offer is shunted aside without expression.

I used to tell my husband that, if he could make me 'understand' something, it would be clear to all the other people in the country.

133

Perhaps nature is our best assurance of immortality.

Campaign behavior for wives: Always be on time. Do as little talking as humanly possible. Lean back in the parade car so everybody can see the president.

Life must be lived and curiosity kept alive. One must never, for whatever reason, turn his back on life.

It takes as much energy to wish as it does to plan.

When you cease to make a contribution, you begin to die.

Old age has deformities enough of its own. It should never add to them the deformity of vice.

In all our contacts it is probably the sense of being really needed and wanted which gives us the greatest satisfaction and creates the most lasting bond.

Hate and force cannot be in just a part of the world without having an effect on the rest of it.

#100

Sometimes I wonder if we shall ever grow up in our politics and say definite things which mean something, or whether we shall always go on using generalities to which everyone can subscribe, and which mean very little.

Ambition is pitiless. Any merit that it cannot use it finds despicable.

I think I lived those years very impersonally. It was almost as though I had erected someone outside myself who was the president's wife. I was lost somewhere deep down inside myself. That is the way I felt and worked until I left the White House.

FRANKLIN D ROOSEVELT

Franklin D Roosevelt (1882 – 1945) was the 32nd President of the United States. He was President during tumultuous times coming to office during the Great Depression and instituted the New Deal to bring about recovery. He was also in office during the attack on Pearl Harbor and the US entry into WW2. He died in office before victory had been secured.

As Americans, we go forward, in the service of our country, by the will of God.

Be sincere; be brief; be seated.

Happiness lies in the joy of achievement and the thrill of creative effort.

I sometimes think that the saving grace of America lies in the fact that the overwhelming majority of Americans are possessed of two great qualities- a sense of humor and a sense of proportion.

If you treat people right they will treat you right - ninety percent of the time.

It is common sense to take a method and try it. If it fails, admit it frankly and try another. But above all, try something.

The constant free flow of communication amount us-enabling the free interchange of ideas-forms the very bloodstream of our nation. It keeps the mind and body of our democracy eternally vital, eternally young.

We cannot always build the future for our youth, but we can build our youth for the future.

We have always known that heedless self-interest was bad morals; we know now that it is bad economics.

We must remember that any oppression, any injustice, any hatred, is a wedge designed to attack our civilization.

Yesterday, December 7, 1941 - a date which will live on in infamy - the United States of America was suddenly and deliberately attacked by naval and air forces of the Empire of Japan.

We defend and we build a way of life, not for America alone, but for all mankind.

First of all, let me assert my firm belief that the only thing we have to fear is fear itself - nameless, unreasoning, unjustified terror which paralyzes needed efforts to convert retreat into advance.

Men are not prisoners of fate, but only prisoners of their own minds.

When you get to the end of your rope, tie a knot and hang on.

A conservative is a man with two perfectly good legs who, however, has never learned to walk forward.

Repetition does not transform a lie into a truth.

The true conservative is the man who has a real concern for injustices and takes thought against the day of reckoning.

In the truest sense, freedom cannot be bestowed; it must be achieved.

Happiness lies not in the mere possession of money. It lies in the joy of achievement, in the thrill of creative effort.

The only thing we have to fear is fear itself.

Democracy cannot succeed unless those who express their choice are prepared to choose wisely. The real safeguard of democracy, therefore, is education.

Nobody will ever deprive the American people of the right to vote except the American people themselves and the only way they could do this is by not voting.

The test of our progress is not whether we add more to the abundance of those who have much it is whether we provide enough for those who have little.

Confidence... thrives on honesty, on honor, on the sacredness of obligations, on faithful protection and on unselfish performance. Without them it cannot live.

There are many ways of going forward, but only one way of standing still.

It isn't sufficient just to want - you've got to ask yourself what you are going to do to get the things you want.

There is a mysterious cycle in human events. To some generations much is given. Of other generations much is expected. This generation of Americans has a rendezvous with destiny.

Human kindness has never weakened the stamina or softened the fiber of a free people. A nation does not have to be cruel to be tough.

We have always held to the hope, the belief, the conviction that there is a better life, a better world, beyond the horizon.

Here is my principle: Taxes shall be levied according to ability to pay. That is the only American principle.

The only limit to our realization of tomorrow will be our doubts of today.

The nation that destroys its soil destroys itself.

I think we consider too much the good luck of the early bird and not enough the bad luck of the early worm.

Competition has been shown to be useful up to a certain point and no further, but cooperation, which is the thing we must strive for today, begins where competition leaves off.

True individual freedom cannot exist without economic security and independence. People who are hungry and out of a job are the stuff of which dictatorships are made.

When you see a rattlesnake poised to strike, you do not wait until he has struck to crush him.

Physical strength can never permanently withstand the impact of spiritual force.

The school is the last expenditure upon which America should be willing to economize.

TEDDY ROOSEVELT

Teddy Roosevelt (1858 – 1919) was the 26th President of the United States, and the youngest at age 42. He helped to reshape the office of the Presidency and the United States role in the world. He was one of the first conservationists and his proposals laid the foundations for the welfare state.

A man who has never gone to school may steal from a freight car; but if he has a university education he may steal the whole railroad.

Aggressive fighting for the right is the greatest sport in the world.

Do what you can, with what you have, where you are.

Don't hit at all if it is honorably possible to avoid hitting; but never hit soft!

Far better it is to dare mighty things, to win glorious triumphs even though checkered by failure, than to rank with those poor spirits who neither enjoy nor suffer much because they live in the gray twilight that knows neither victory nor defeat.

I wish to preach, not the doctrine of ignoble ease, but the doctrine of the strenuous life.

In a civilized and cultivated country, wild animals only continue to exist at all when preserved by sportsmen.

It behooves every man to remember that the work of the critic is of altogether secondary importance, and that in the end, progress is accomplished by the man who does things.

No, I'm not a good shot, but I shoot often.

Patriotism means to stand by the country. It does not mean to stand by the president.

The decisions of the courts on economic and social questions depend on their economic and social philosophy.

The United States does not have a choice as to whether or not is will or will not play a great part in the world. Fate has made that choice for us. The only question is whether we will play the part well or badly.

The wild life of today is not ours to do with as we please. The original stock was given to us in trust for the benefit both of the present and the future. We must render an accounting of this trust to those who come after us.

To announce that there must be no criticism of the president, right or wrong - is not only unpatriotic and servile, but is morally treasonable to the American public.

To educate a man in mind and not in morals is to educate a menace to society.

When you play, play hard; when you work, don't play at all.

Whenever you are asked if you can do a job, tell 'em, 'Certainly I can!' Then get busy and find out how to do it.

No man is justified in doing evil on the ground of expediency.

Justice consists not in being neutral between right and wrong, but in finding out the right and upholding it, wherever found, against the wrong.

We are face to face with our destiny and we must meet it with high and resolute courage. For us is the life of action, of strenuous performance of duty; let us live in the harness, striving mightily; let us rather run the risk of wearing out than rusting out.

The death-knell of the republic had rung as soon as the active power became lodged in the hands of those who sought, not to do justice to all citizens, rich and poor alike, but to stand for one special class and for its interests as opposed to the interests of others.

The conservation of our natural resources and their proper use constitute the fundamental problem which underlies almost every other problem of our national life.

The most practical kind of politics is the politics of decency.

The nation behaves well if it treats the natural resources as assets which it must turn over to the next generation increased, and not impaired, in value.

There is a homely old adage which runs: "Speak softly and carry a big stick; you will go far." If the American nation will speak softly, and yet build and keep at a pitch of the highest training a thoroughly efficient navy, the Monroe Doctrine will go far.

Far and away the best prize that life offers is the chance to work hard at work worth doing.

Let us speak courteously, deal fairly, and keep ourselves armed and ready.

No foreign policy-no matter how ingenious-has any chance of success if it is born in the minds of few and carried in the hearts of many.

We cannot afford merely to sit down and deplore the evils of city life as inevitable, when cities are constantly growing, both absolutely and relatively. We must set ourselves vigorously about the task of improving them; and this task is now well begun.

Wars are, of course, as a rule to be avoided; but they are far better than certain kinds of peace.

The most important single ingredient in the formula of success is knowing how to get along with people.

People ask the difference between a leader and a boss. The leader works in the open, and the boss in covert. The leader leads, and the boss drives.

Far better is it to dare mighty things, to win glorious triumphs, even though checkered by failure than to rank with those poor spirits who neither enjoy much nor suffer much, because they live in a gray twilight that knows not victory nor defeat.

In any moment of decision, the best thing you can do is the right thing, the next best thing is the wrong thing, and the worst thing you can do is nothing.

Every immigrant who comes here should be required within five years to learn English or leave the country.

When they call the roll in the Senate, the senators do not know whether to answer "present" or "not guilty."

Speak softly and carry a big stick; you will go far.

Keep your eyes on the stars, and your feet on the ground.

Believe you can and you're halfway there.

If you could kick the person in the pants responsible for most of your trouble, you wouldn't sit for a month.

Nobody cares how much you know, until they know how much you care.

It is only through labor and painful effort, by grim energy and resolute courage that we move on to better things.

A vote is like a rifle; its usefulness depends upon the character of the user.

Get action. Seize the moment. Man was never intended to become an oyster.

The best executive is one who has sense enough to pick good people to do what he wants done, and self-restraint enough to keep from meddling with them while they do it.

The things that will destroy America are prosperity-at-any-price, peace-at-any-price, safety-first instead of duty-first, the love of soft living, and the get-rich-quick theory of life.

Great thoughts speak only to the thoughtful mind, but great actions speak to all mankind.

Never throughout history has a man who lived a life of ease left a name worth remembering.

A typical vice of American politics is the avoidance of saying anything real on real issues.

BABE RUTH

Babe Ruth (1895 – 1948) was a professional baseball player and is considered the greatest player of all time. His career in Major League Baseball extended to 22 seasons. He achieved his greatest popularity as a slugging outfielder for the New York Yankees. Some of his records stand to this day.

The way a team plays as a whole determines its success. You may have the greatest bunch of individual stars in the world, but if they don't play together, the club won't be worth a dime.

You just can't beat the person who never gives up.

I've heard people say that the trouble with the world is that we haven't enough great leaders. I think we haven't enough great followers. I have stood side by side with great thinkers - surgeons, engineers, economists; people who deserve a great following - and have heard the crowd cheer me instead.

I didn't mean to hit the umpire with the dirt, but I did mean to hit that bastard in the stands.

I had only one superstition. I made sure to touch all the bases when I hit a home run.

Never let the fear of striking out get in your way.

Yesterday's home runs don't win today's games.

Reading isn't good for a ballplayer. Not good for his eyes. If my eyes went bad even a little bit I couldn't hit home runs. So I gave up reading.

If I'd just tried for them dinky singles I could've batted around .600.

If it wasn't for baseball, I'd be in either the penitentiary or the cemetery.

All I can tell them is pick a good one and sock it. I get back to the dugout and they ask me what it was I hit and I tell them I don't know except it looked good.

Don't ever forget two things I'm going to tell you. One, don't believe everything that's written about you. Two, don't pick up too many check

I won't be happy until we have every boy in America between the ages of six and sixteen wearing a glove and swinging a bat.

Gee, its lonesome in the outfield. It's hard to keep awake with nothing to do.

All ballplayers should quit when it starts to feel as if all the baselines run uphill.

How to hit home runs: I swing as hard as I can, and I try to swing right through the ball... The harder you grip the bat, the more you can swing it through the ball, and the farther the ball will go. I swing big, with everything I've got. I hit big or I miss big. I like to live as big as I can.

Baseball was, is and always will be to me the best game in the world. I'll promise to go easier on drinking and to get to bed earlier, but not for you, fifty thousand dollars, or two-hundred and fifty thousand dollars will I give up women. They're too much fun.

I never heard a crowd boo a homer, but I've heard plenty of boos after a strikeout.

A man who knows he's making money for other people ought to get some of the profits he brings in.

Life is a game like any other; we just don't take it as seriously.

Heroes get remembered, but legends never die.

I don't need to know where the green is. Where is the golf course?

#123

Don't be afraid to take advice. There's always something new to learn.

#124

A part of control is learning to correct your own weaknesses. The person doesn't live who was born with everything. Sometimes he has one weak point, generally he has several. The first thing is to know your faults. And then take on a systematic plan of correcting them. You know the old saying about a chain only being as strong as its weakest link. The same can be said in the chain of skills a man forges.

CARL SAGAN

Carl Sagan (1934 – 96) was an astronomer, cosmologist and astrophysicist though is best known as a communicator and popularizer in astronomy. He narrated and co-wrote 'Cosmos: A Personal Voyage' which is the most popular series in the history of American public broadcasting having been watched by 500 million people worldwide.

Somewhere, something incredible is waiting to be known.

We can judge our progress by the courage of our questions and the depth of our answers, our willingness to embrace what is true rather than what feels good.

If you wish to make an apple pie from scratch, you must first invent the universe

Every one of us is, in the cosmic perspective, precious. If a human disagrees with you, let him live. In a hundred billion galaxies, you will not find another.

The nitrogen in our DNA, the calcium in our teeth, the iron in our blood, the carbon in our apple pies were made in the interiors of collapsing stars. We are made of star stuff.

Imagination will often carry us to worlds that never were, but without it we go nowhere

Science is not only compatible with spirituality; it is a profound source of spirituality.

It pays to keep an open mind, but not so open your brains fall out.

The universe is a pretty big place. If it's just us, seems like an awful waste of space.

We are like butterflies who flutter for a day and think it is forever.

Absence of evidence is not evidence of absence.

Skeptical scrutiny is the means, in both science and religion, by which deep thoughts can be winnowed from deep nonsense.

We live in a society exquisitely dependent on science and technology, in which hardly anyone knows anything about science and technology.

One glance at a book and you hear the voice of another person, perhaps someone dead for 1,000 years. To read is to voyage through time.

Who is more humble? The scientist who looks at the universe with an open mind and accepts whatever the universe has to teach us, or somebody who says everything in this book must be considered the literal truth and never mind the fallibility of all the human beings involved?

Science is a way of thinking much more than it is a body of knowledge.

A celibate clergy is an especially good idea, because it tends to suppress any hereditary propensity toward fanaticism.

The universe seems neither benign nor hostile, merely indifferent.

The fact that some geniuses were laughed at does not imply that all who are laughed at are geniuses.

Books permit us to voyage through time, to tap the wisdom of our ancestors.

A tiny blue dot set in a sunbeam. Here it is. That's where we live. That's home. We humans are one species and this is our world. It is our responsibility to cherish it. Of all the worlds in our solar system, the only one so far as we know, graced by life.

Those worlds in space are as countless as all the grains of sand on all the beaches of the earth.

It is the tension between creativity and skepticism that has produced the stunning and unexpected findings of science.

The size and age of the Cosmos are beyond ordinary human understanding. Lost somewhere between immensity and eternity is our tiny planetary home.

Far better it seems to me, in our vulnerability, is to look death in the eye and to be grateful every day for the brief but magnificent opportunity that life provides.

STEVEN SPIELBERG

Steven Spielberg (1946 -) is a Hollywood director and producer. His career has spanned more than 40 years and his films include some of the most popular of all time. He received the Academy Award for Best Director for Schindler's List and Saving Private Ryan. He is the highest grossing director of all time.

I dream for a living.

I'd rather direct than produce. Any day. And twice on Sunday.

I never felt comfortable with myself, because I was never part of the majority. I always felt awkward and shy and on the outside of the momentum of my friends' lives.

Technology can be our best friend, and technology can also be the biggest party pooper of our lives. It interrupts our own story, interrupts our ability to have a thought or a daydream, to imagine something wonderful, because we're too busy bridging the walk from the cafeteria back to the office on the cell phone.

The delicate balance of mentoring someone is not creating them in your own image, but giving them the opportunity to create themselves.

There is a fine line between censorship and good taste and moral responsibility.

I have never before, in my long and eclectic career, been gifted with such an abundance of natural beauty as I experienced filming 'War Horse' on Dartmoor.

You have many years ahead of you to create the dreams that we can't even imagine dreaming. You have done more for the collective unconscious of this planet than you will ever know.

The only time I have a good hunch the audience is going to be there is when I make the sequel to 'Jurassic Park' or I make another Indiana Jones movie. I know I've got a good shot at getting an audience on opening night. Everything else that is striking out into new territory is a crap shoot.

I don't think that anybody in any war thinks of themselves as a hero. The minute anybody presumes that they are heroes, they get their boots taken away from them and buried in the sand.

I think documentaries are the greatest way to educate an entire generation that doesn't often look back to learn anything about the history that provided a safe haven for so many of us today.

Social media has taken over in America to such an extreme that to get my own kids to look back a week in their history is a miracle, let alone 100 years.

This whole thing about reality television to me is really indicative of America saying we're not satisfied just watching television, we want to star in our own TV shows. We want you to discover us and put us in your own TV show, and we want television to be about us, finally.

The public has an appetite for anything about imagination - anything that is as far away from reality as is creatively possible.

'E.T.' began with me trying to write a story about my parents' divorce.

I believe in 3D for certain kinds of films. I certainly believe in using 3D for all things in animation because animation has such clarity and so much depth of focus. It worked great with 'Avatar' because 70 percent of that film is animated.

MARK TWAIN

Mark Twain (1835 – 1910) was a writer, entrepreneur, public speaker and adventurer. His novel 'The Adventures of Huckleberry Finn' has been called the great American novel

It ain't what you don't know that gets you into trouble. It's what you know for sure that just ain't so.

Get your facts first, then you can distort them as you please.

The trouble ain't that there is too many fools, but that the lightning ain't distributed right.

Twenty years from now you will be more disappointed by the things that you didn't do than by the ones you did do. So throw off the bowlines. Sail away from the safe harbor. Catch the trade winds in your sails. Explore. Dream. Discover.

It's not the size of the dog in the fight, it's the size of the fight in the dog.

I was seldom able to see an opportunity until it had ceased to be one.

Patriot: the person who can holler the loudest without knowing what he is hollering about.

A man's character may be learned from the adjectives which he habitually uses in conversation

Patriotism is supporting your country all the time, and your government when it deserves it.

When red-haired people are above a certain social grade their hair is auburn.

The more things are forbidden, the more popular they become.

It is easier to stay out than get out.

Action speaks louder than words but not nearly as often.

The secret of getting ahead is getting started. The secret of getting started is breaking your complex overwhelming tasks into small manageable tasks, and then starting on the first one.

To succeed in life, you need two things: ignorance and confidence.

The only way to keep your health is to eat what you don't want, drink what you don't like, and do what you'd rather not.

When you fish for love, bait with your heart, not your brain.

When angry, count to four. When very angry, swear.

But who prays for Satan? Who, in eighteen centuries, has had the common humanity to pray for the one sinner that needed it most?

Substitute "damn" every time you're inclined to write "very"; your editor will delete it and the writing will be just as it should be.

Don't go around saying the world owes you a living; the world owes you nothing; it was here first.

Life does not consist mainly, or even largely, of facts and happenings. It consists mainly of the storm of thought that is forever flowing through one's head.

Any emotion, if it is sincere, is involuntary.

Life would be infinitely happier if we could only be born at the age of eighty and gradually approach eighteen.

What a wee little part of a person's life are his acts and his words! His real life is led in his head, and is known to none but himself.

Buy land, they're not making it anymore

When I was younger I could remember anything, whether it happened or not.

It is better to deserve honors and not have them than to have them and not to deserve them.

The human race has only one really effective weapon and that is laughter.

The radical of one century is the conservative of the next. The radical invents the views. When he has worn them out, the conservative adopts them.

Good breeding consists of concealing how much we think of ourselves and how little we think of the other person.

There are basically two types of people. People who accomplish things, and people who claim to have accomplished things. The first group is less crowded.

We have the best government that money can buy.

Courage is resistance to fear, mastery of fear - not absence of fear.

When people do not respect us we are sharply offended; yet in his private heart no man much respects himself.

Thousands of geniuses live and die undiscovered -- either by themselves or by others.

Books are for people who wish they were somewhere else.

In the real world, nothing happens at the right place at the right time. It is the job of journalists and historians to correct that.

Don't part with your illusions. When they are gone you may still exist, but you have ceased to live.

Man is the only creature who has a nasty mind.

Only kings, presidents, editors, and people with tapeworms have the right to use the editorial "we".

A habit cannot be tossed out the window; it must be coaxed down the stairs a step at a time.

A classic is something that everybody wants to have read and nobody wants to read.

Always do right. This will gratify some people and astonish the rest.

Do not put off till tomorrow what can be put off till day-after-tomorrow just as well.

Really great people make you feel that you, too, can become great.

The fear of death follows from the fear of life. A man who lives fully is prepared to die at any time.

Under certain circumstances, profanity provides a relief denied even to prayer.

Conservatism is the blind and fear-filled worship of dead radicals.

It is curious - curious that physical courage should be so common in the world, and moral courage so rare.

If you tell the truth you don't have to remember anything.

The man who does not read good books has no advantage over the man who cannot read them.

If Christ were here now there is one thing he would not be - a Christian.

Heaven goes by favor; if it went by merit, you would stay out and your dog would go in.

In Paris they simply stared when I spoke to them in French; I never did succeed in making those idiots understand their own language.

Broad, wholesome, charitable views ... cannot be acquired by vegetating in one's little corner of the earth.

After all these years I see that I was mistaken about Eve in the beginning; it is better to live outside the Garden with her than inside it without her.

Good friends, good books and a sleepy conscience: this is the ideal life.

A man's private thought can never be a lie; what he thinks, is to him the truth, always.

JOHN UPDIKE

John Updike (1932 – 2009) was a novelist and a poet who published over twenty novels as well as poetry and children's books. He is most famous for his 'Rabbit' series of novels for which he won two Pulitzer Prizes in 1982 and 1990.

Writers may be disreputable, incorrigible, early to decay or late to bloom but they dare to go it alone.

Swallow a toad in the morning and you will encounter nothing more disgusting the rest of the day.

Existence itself does not feel horrible; it feels like an ecstasy, rather, which we have only to be still to experience.

The true New Yorker secretly believes that people living anywhere else have to be, in some sense, kidding.

Being naked approaches being revolutionary; going barefoot is mere populism.

It is easy to love people in memory; the hard thing is to love them when they are there in front of you.

Dreams come true. Without that possibility, nature would not incite us to have them.

Chaos is God's body. Order is the Devil's chains

Celebrity is a mask that eats into the face.

Is not the decisive difference between comedy and tragedy that tragedy denies us another chance?

How do you write women so well? I think of a man and I take away reason and accountability.

It rots a writer's brain, it cretinises you. You say the same thing again and again, and when you do that happily you're well on the way to being a cretin. Or a politician.

Possession diminishes perception of value, immediately.

Suspect each moment, for it is a thief, tiptoeing away with more than it brings.

I think "taste" is a social concept and not an artistic one.

That a marriage ends is less than ideal; but all things end under heaven, and if temporality is held to be invalidating, then nothing real succeeds.

The great thing about the dead, they make space.

The inner spaces that a good story lets us enter are the old apartments of religion.

Each morning my characters greet me with misty faces willing, though chilled, to muster for another day's progress through the dazzling quicksand the marsh of blank paper.

Sex is like money; only too much is enough.

All vagrants think they're on a quest. At least at first.

Life, just as we first thought, is playing grownup.

Perfectionism is the enemy of creation, as extreme self-solitude is the enemy of well-being.

Inch by inch.
Life is a cinch.
Yard by yard.
Life is hard.

GORE VIDAL

Gore Vidal (1925 – 2012) was a novelist and essayist and applied himself to many subjects, most notably sex, politics and religion. He was an intellectual known for his wit and polished writings and was frequently to be seen on television chat shows. The French newspaper 'Le Figaro' described him as 'the killjoy of America.'.

Andy Warhol is the only genius I've ever known with an IQ of 60.

A good deed never goes unpunished.

All children alarm their parents, if only because you are forever expecting to encounter yourself.

Apparently, a democracy is a place where numerous elections are held at great cost without issues and with interchangeable candidates.

Fifty percent of people won't vote, and fifty percent don't read newspapers. I hope it's the same fifty percent.

Some writers take to drink, others take to audiences.

A narcissist is someone better looking than you are.

It is not enough to succeed. Others must fail.

Never pass up a chance to have sex or appear on television.

Half of the American people have never read a newspaper. Half never voted for President. One hopes it is the same half.

The genius of our ruling class is that it has kept a majority of the people from ever questioning the inequity of a system where most people drudge along, paying heavy taxes for which they get nothing in return.

The more money an American accumulates, the less interesting he becomes.

The four most beautiful words in our common language: I told you so.

Congress no longer declares war or makes budgets. So that's the end of the constitution as a working machine.

It's easy to sustain a relationship when sex plays no part, and impossible, I have observed, when it does.

Whenever a friend succeeds, a little something in me dies.

Never have children, only grandchildren.

There is no human problem which could not be solved if people would simply do as I advise.

Write something, even if it's just a suicide note.

We should stop going around babbling about how we're the greatest democracy on earth, when we're not even a democracy. We are a sort of militarized republic.

As the age of television progresses the Reagan's will be the rule, not the exception. To be perfect for television is all a President has to be these days.

Sex is. There is nothing more to be done about it. Sex builds no roads, writes no novels and sex certainly gives no meaning to anything in life but itself.

Think of the earth as a living organism that is being attacked by billions of bacteria whose numbers double every forty years. Either the host dies, or the virus dies, or both die.

It is not enough to succeed. Others must fail.

Any American who is prepared to run for president should automatically by definition be disqualified from ever doing so.

Democracy is supposed to give you the feeling of choice like, Painkiller X and Painkiller Y. But they're both just aspirin.

Envy is the central fact of American life.

The United States was founded by the brightest people in the country — and we haven't seen them since.

Every four years the naive half who vote are encouraged to believe that if we can elect a really nice man or woman President everything will be all right. But it won't be.

There is no such thing as a homosexual or a heterosexual person. There are only homo- or heterosexual acts. Most people are a mixture of impulses if not practices.

JAMES MCNEILL WHISTLER

James McNeill Whistler (1834 – 1903) was an American painter who lived for many years in the United Kingdom. He was one of the main protagonists of the 'Aesthetic Movement' which pursued an 'Art for Art's sake' philosophy. He was a leading proponent of Tonalism which was a significant influence on many artists.

Paint should not be applied thick. It should be like a breath on the surface of a pane of glass.

Art happens – no hovel is safe from it, no prince can depend on it, the vastest intelligence cannot bring it about.

Mauve? Mauve is just pink trying to be purple.

Two and two continue to make four, in spite of the whine of the amateur for three, or the cry of the critic for five.

As far as painting is concerned there is only Degas and myself.

A picture is finished when all trace of the means used to bring about the end has disappeared.

To say to the painter that Nature is to be taken as she is, is to say to the player that he may sit on the piano.

An artist is not paid for his labor but for his vision.

Nature is usually wrong.

I can't tell you if genius is hereditary, because heaven has granted me no offspring.

If other people are going to talk, conversation becomes impossible.

People will forgive anything but beauty and talent. So I am doubly unpardonable.

The world is divided into two classes - invalids and nurses.

It takes a long time for a man to look like his portrait.

You shouldn't say it is not good. You should say, you do not like it; and then, you know, you're perfectly safe.

All true artists, whether they know it or not, create from a place of no-mind, from inner stillness.

Industry in art is a necessity—not a virtue—and any evidence of the same, in the production, is a blemish, not a quality; a proof, not of achievement, but of absolutely insufficient work, for work alone will efface the footsteps of work.

George Washington

George Washington (1732 – 99) was the first President of the United States and one of the Founding Fathers. He was also the Commander in Chief during the American Revolutionary War to gain independence from Great Britain. As President he pursued liberty and the establishment of American nationalism.

My mother was the most beautiful woman I ever saw. All I am I owe to my mother. I attribute all my success in life to the moral, intellectual and physical education I received from her.

If the freedom of speech is taken away then dumb and silent we may be led, like sheep to the slaughter.

It is better to be alone than in bad company.

Observe good faith and justice toward all nations. Cultivate peace and harmony with all.

Liberty, when it begins to take root, is a plant of rapid growth.

To be prepared for war is one of the most effective means of preserving peace.

True friendship is a plant of slow growth, and must undergo and withstand the shocks of adversity, before it is entitled to the appellation.

Labor to keep alive in your breast that little spark of celestial fire, called conscience.

Happiness and moral duty are inseparably connected.

The time is near at hand which must determine whether Americans are to be free men or slaves.

We should not look back unless it is to derive useful lessons from past errors, and for the purpose of profiting by dearly bought experience.

It is better to offer no excuse than a bad one.

My first wish is to see this plague of mankind, war, banished from the earth.

Discipline is the soul of an army. It makes small numbers formidable; procures success to the weak, and esteem to all.

Few men have virtue to withstand the highest bidder.

The Constitution is the guide which I never will abandon.

The basis of our political system is the right of the people to make and to alter their constitutions of government.

Arbitrary power is most easily established on the ruins of liberty abused to licentiousness.

Truth will ultimately prevail where there is pains to bring it to light.

Experience teaches us that it is much easier to prevent an enemy from posting themselves than it is to dislodge them after they have got possession.

I beg you be persuaded that no one would be more zealous than myself to establish effectual barriers against the horrors of spiritual tyranny, and every species of religious persecution.

Let your Discourse with Men of Business be Short and Comprehensive.

Let us raise a standard to which the wise and honest can repair; the rest is in the hands of God.

There is nothing which can better deserve your patronage, than the promotion of science and literature. Knowledge is in every country the surest basis of public happiness.

Worry is the interest paid by those who borrow trouble.

When we assumed the Soldier, we did not lay aside the Citizen.

Laws made by common consent must not be trampled on by individuals.

Associate with men of good quality if you esteem your own reputation; for it is better to be alone than in bad company.

If we desire to avoid insult, we must be able to repel it; if we desire to secure peace, one of the most powerful instruments of our rising prosperity, it must be known, that we are at all times ready for War.

There can be no greater error than to expect, or calculate, upon real favors from nation to nation. It is an illusion which experience must cure, which a just pride ought to discard.

It will be found an unjust and unwise jealousy to deprive a man of his natural liberty upon the supposition he may abuse it.

Over grown military establishments are under any form of government inauspicious to liberty, and are to be regarded as particularly hostile to republican liberty.

I hope I shall possess firmness and virtue enough to maintain what I consider the most enviable of all titles, the character of an honest man.

A slender acquaintance with the world must convince every man that actions, not words, are the true criterion of the attachment of friends.

Let your heart feel for the afflictions and distress of everyone, and let your hand give in proportion to your purse.

My observation is that whenever one person is found adequate to the discharge of a duty... it is worse executed by two persons, and scarcely done at all if three or more are employed therein.

The very atmosphere of firearms anywhere and everywhere restrains evil interference - they deserve a place of honor with all that's good.

The foolish and wicked practice of profane cursing and swearing is a vice so mean and low that every person of sense and character detests and despises it.

ORSON WELLES

Orson Welles (1915 – 85) was an actor, director and producer. He first found fame as the director of a radio broadcast of War of the Worlds, which caused widespread panic. He is best remembered for what are regarded as some of the greatest films ever made which include Citizen Kane, The Third Man and The Magnificent Ambersons.

We're born alone, we live alone, we die alone. Only through our love and friendship can we create the illusion for the moment that we're not alone.

Create your own visual style... let it be unique for yourself and yet identifiable for others.

Ask not what you can do for your country. Ask what's for lunch.

Nobody gets justice. People only get good luck or bad luck.

If you want a happy ending that depends, of course, on where you stop your story.

Popularity should be no scale for the election of politicians. If it would depend on popularity, Donald Duck and The Muppets would take seats in senate.

I was spoiled in a very strange way as a child, because everybody told me, from the moment I was able to hear, that I was absolutely marvelous, and I never heard a discouraging word for years, you see. I didn't know what was ahead of me.

My doctor told me to stop having intimate dinners for four. Unless there are three other people.

I have a great love and respect for religion, great love and respect for atheism. What I hate is agnosticism, people who do not choose.

If there hadn't been women we'd still be squatting in a cave eating raw meat, because we made civilization in order to impress our girlfriends.

I have the terrible feeling that, because I am wearing a white beard and am sitting in the back of the theatre, you expect me to tell you the truth about something. These are the cheap seats, not Mount Sinai.

Nobody who takes on anything big and tough can afford to be modest.

When you are down and out something always turns up - and it is usually the noses of your friends.

Race hate isn't human nature; race hate is the abandonment of human nature.

The notion of directing a film is the invention of critics - the whole eloquence of cinema is achieved in the editing room.

I hate television. I hate it as much as peanuts. But I can't stop eating peanuts.

The enemy of society is middle class and the enemy of life is middle age.

Personally, I don't like a girlfriend to have a husband. If she'll fool her husband, I figure she'll fool me.

Everybody denies I am a genius - but nobody ever called me one.

Man is a rational animal who always loses his temper when called upon to act in accordance with the dictates of reason.

My mother and father were both much more remarkable than any story of mine can make them. They seem to me just mythically wonderful.

#135 When people accept breaking the law as normal, something happens to the whole society.

The two things you cannot do effectively on stage are pray and copulate.

Hollywood is the only industry, even taking in soup companies, which does not have laboratories for the purpose of experimentation.

If I ever own a restaurant, I will never allow the waiters to ask if the diners like their dishes. Particularly when they're talking.

I prefer people who rock the boat to people who jump out

Style is knowing who you are, what you want to say, and not giving a damn

There are three intolerable things in life - cold coffee, lukewarm champagne, and overexcited women

OPRAH WINFREY

Oprah Winfrey (1954 -) is a chat show host, actress and philanthropist. The Oprah Winfrey Show, which ran from 1986 – 2011, was the highest ranked talk show of its time. She is believed to be the wealthiest African American and, according to some assessments, the most influential woman in the world.

Think like a queen. A queen is not afraid to fail. Failure is another steppingstone to greatness.

The more you praise and celebrate your life, the more there is in life to celebrate.

The biggest adventure you can take is to live the life of your dreams.

Be thankful for what you have; you'll end up having more. If you concentrate on what you don't have, you will never, ever have enough.

Lots of people want to ride with you in the limo, but what you want is someone who will take the bus with you when the limo breaks down.

Surround yourself with only people who are going to lift you higher.

I believe that every single event in life happens in an opportunity to choose love over fear.

I still have my feet on the ground, I just wear better shoes.

Real integrity is doing the right thing, knowing that nobody's going to know whether you did it or not.

Where there is no struggle, there is no strength.

You know you are on the road to success if you would do your job, and not be paid for it.

I have a lot of things to prove to myself. One is that I can live my life fearlessly.

I'm black, I don't feel burdened by it and I don't think it's a huge responsibility. It's part of who I am. It does not define me.

It isn't until you come to a spiritual understanding of who you are - not necessarily a religious feeling, but deep down, the spirit within - that you can begin to take control.

Cheers to a new year and another chance for us to get it right.

Passion is energy. Feel the power that comes from focusing on what excites you.

If you come to fame not understanding who you are, it will define who you are.

So go ahead. Fall down. The world looks different from the ground.

My philosophy is that not only are you responsible for your life, but doing the best at this moment puts you I the best place for the next moment.

I don't think you ever stop giving. I really don't. I think it's an on-going process. And it's not just about being able to write a check. It's being able to touch somebody's life.

I don't think of myself as a poor deprived ghetto girl who made good. I think of myself as somebody who from an early age knew I was responsible for myself, and I had to make good.

Understand that the right to choose your own path is a sacred privilege. Use it. Dwell in possibility.

Books were my pass to personal freedom. I learned to read at age three, and soon discovered there was a whole world to conquer that went beyond our farm in Mississippi.

I feel that luck is preparation meeting opportunity.

The struggle of my life created empathy - I could relate to pain, being abandoned, having people not love me.

Breathe. Let go. And remind yourself that this very moment is the only one you know you have for sure.

The whole point of being alive is to evolve into the complete person you were intended to be.

Do the one thing you think you cannot do. Fail at it. Try again. Do better the second time. The only people who never tumble are those who never mount the high wire. This is your moment. Own it.

The greatest discovery of all time is that a person can change his future by merely changing his attitude.

Follow your instincts. That's where true wisdom manifests itself.

Turn your wounds into wisdom.

It's much easier for me to make major life, multi-million dollar decisions, than it is to decide on a carpet for my front porch. That's the truth.

I remember a specific moment, watching my grandmother hang the clothes on the line, and her saying to me, 'you are going to have to learn to do this,' and me being in that space of awareness and knowing that my life would not be the same as my grandmother's life.

The thing you fear most has no power. Your fear of it is what has the power. Facing the truth really will set you free.

Excellence is the best deterrent to racism or sexism.

For everyone of us that succeeds, it's because there's somebody there to show you the way out.

As you become more clear about who you really are, you'll be better able to decide what is best for you - the first time around.

Biology is the least of what makes someone a mother.

I don't believe in failure. It is not failure if you enjoyed the process.

MALCOM X

Malcolm X (1925 – 65) was an African American Muslim minister and a civil rights activist. He was more aggressive in his promotion of black rights than some others and is considered the most influential African American. He was largely responsible for the conversion of many black Americans to Islam.

You're not to be so blind with patriotism that you can't face reality. Wrong is wrong, no matter who does it or says it.

We do not condemn the preachers as an individual but we condemn what they teach. We urge that the preachers teach the truth, to teach our people the one important guiding rule of conduct - unity of purpose.

It's just like when you've got some coffee that's too black, which means it's too strong. What do you do? You integrate it with cream, you make it weak. But if you pour too much cream in it, you won't even know you ever had coffee. It used to be hot, it becomes cool. It used to be strong, it becomes weak. It used to wake you up, now it puts you to sleep.

I don't even call it violence when it's in self defense; I call it intelligence.

If violence is wrong in America, violence is wrong abroad. If it is wrong to be violent defending black women and black children and black babies and black men, then it is wrong for America to draft us, and make us violent abroad in defense of her. And if it is right for America to draft us, and teach us how to be violent in defense of her, then it is right for you and me to do whatever is necessary to defend our own people right here in this country.

Nonviolence is fine as long as it works.

I am for violence if non-violence means we continue postponing a solution to the American black man's problem just to avoid violence.

There can be no black-white unity until there is first some black unity.... We cannot think of uniting with others, until after we have first united among ourselves. We cannot think of being acceptable to others until we have first proven acceptable to ourselves.

We black men have a hard enough time in our own struggle for justice, and already have enough enemies as it is, to make the drastic mistake of attacking each other and adding more weight to an already unbearable load.

It is a time for martyrs now, and if I am to be one, it will be for the cause of brotherhood. That's the only thing that can save this country.

My Alma mater was books, a good library... I could spend the rest of my life reading, just satisfying my curiosity.

Education is the passport to the future, for tomorrow belongs to those who prepare for it today.

I have often reflected upon the new vistas that reading opened to me. I knew right there in prison that reading had changed forever the course of my life. As I see it today, the ability to read awoke in me some long dormant craving to be mentally alive.

Without education, you are not going anywhere in this world.

We declare our right on this earth to be a human being, to be respected as a human being, to be given the rights of a human being in this society, on this earth, in this day, which we intend to bring into existence by any means necessary.

I've never seen a sincere white man, not when it comes to helping black people. Usually things like this are done by white people to benefit themselves. The white man's primary interest is not to elevate the thinking of black people, or to waken black people, or white people either. The white man is interested in the black man only to the extent that the black man is of use to him. The white man's interest is to make money, to exploit.

I believe in human beings, and that all human beings should be respected as such, regardless of their color.

Nobody can give you freedom. Nobody can give you equality or justice or anything. If you're a man, you take it.

Power in defense of freedom is greater than power in behalf of tyranny, because the power of a just cause is based on conviction, and leads to resolute and uncompromising action.

If you're not ready to die for it, put the word "freedom" out of your vocabulary.

When a person places the proper value on freedom, there is nothing under the sun that he will not do to acquire that freedom. Whenever you hear a man saying he wants freedom, but in the next breath he is going to tell you what he won't do to get it, or what he doesn't believe in doing in order to get it, he doesn't believe in freedom. A man who believes in freedom will do anything under the sun to acquire... or preserve his freedom.

The only way we'll get freedom for ourselves is to identify ourselves with every oppressed people in the world. We are blood brothers to the people of Brazil, Venezuelan Haiti and Cuba.

You don't have to be a man to fight for freedom. All you have to do is to be an intelligent human being.

I believe in a religion that believes in freedom. Any time I have to accept a religion that won't let me fight a battle for my people, I say to hell with that religion.

I believe that it would be almost impossible to find anywhere in America a black man who has lived further down in the mud of human society than I have; or a black man who has been any more ignorant than I have; or a black man who has suffered more anguish during his life than I have. But it is only after the deepest darkness that the greatest joy can come; it is only after slavery and prison that the sweetest appreciation of freedom can come.

The day that the black man takes an uncompromising step and realizes that he's within his rights, when his own freedom is being jeopardized, to use any means necessary to bring about his freedom or put a halt to that injustice, I don't think he'll be by himself.

I believe in the brotherhood of all men, but I don't believe in wasting brotherhood on anyone who doesn't want to practice it with me. Brotherhood is a two-way street.

#138

I don't see an American Dream, I see an American Nightmare.

History is a people's memory, and without a memory, man is demoted to the lower animals.

You show me a capitalist, and I'll show you a bloodsucker.

It is impossible for capitalism to survive, primarily because the system of capitalism needs some blood to suck. Capitalism used to be like an eagle, but now it's more like a vulture. It used to be strong enough to go and suck anybody's blood whether they were strong or not. But now it has become more cowardly, like the vulture, and it can only suck the blood of the helpless. As the nations of the world free themselves, the capitalism has less victims, less to suck, and it becomes weaker and weaker. It's only a matter of time in my opinion before it will collapse completely.

#139

The media's the most powerful entity on earth. They have the power to make the innocent guilty and to make the guilty innocent, and that's power. Because they control the minds of the masses.

The war of Armageddon has already started... God is using his many weapons. He is sending hurricanes so fast that [the blue-eyed devils] can't name them. He is drowning them in floods and causing their cars to crash and their airplanes cannot stay up in the sky. Their boats are sinking because Allah controls all things and he is using all methods to begin to wipe the devils off the planet, [and] the enemy is dying of diseases that have never been so deadly.

I'm the man you think you are.... If you want to know what I'll do, figure out what you'll do. I'll do the same thing--only more of it.

I'm for truth, no matter who tells it. I'm for justice, no matter who it's for or against.

Truth is on the side of the oppressed.

Don't be in a hurry to condemn because he doesn't do what you do or think as you think or as fast. There was a time when you didn't know what you know today.

Be peaceful, be courteous, obey the law, respect everyone; but if someone puts his hand on you, send him to the cemetery.

A man who stands for nothing will fall for anything.

Stumbling is not falling.

There is no better than adversity. Every defeat, every heartbreak, every loss, contains its own seed, its own lesson on how to improve your performance the next time.

Power never takes a back step - only in the face of more power.

The future belongs to those who prepare for it today.

If you have no critics you'll likely have no success.

In all our deeds, the proper value and respect for time determines success or failure.

Usually when people are sad, they don't do anything. They just cry over their condition. But when they get angry, they bring about a change.

You can't separate peace from freedom because no one can be at peace unless he has his freedom.

Time is on the side of the oppressed today, it's against the oppressor. Truth is on the side of the oppressed today, it's against the oppressor. You don't need anything else.

Sitting at the table doesn't make you a diner, unless you eat some of what's on that plate. Being here in America doesn't make you an American. Being born here in America doesn't make you an American.

ONE LAST THING...

If you enjoyed this book or found it useful I'd be very grateful if you'd post a short review on Amazon. Your support really does make a difference and I read all the reviews personally so I can get your feedback and make this book even better.

If you'd like to leave a review then all you need to do is click the review link on this book's Amazon page.

M. Prefontaine

Made in the USA
Las Vegas, NV
30 May 2021

23903317R00105